The Hawaiian Poetry
of Religion and Politics

The Hawaiian Poetry of Religion and Politics

Some Religio-Political Concepts in Postcontact Literature

JOHN CHARLOT

MONOGRAPH SERIES, NO. 5

published by
The Institute for Polynesian Studies
funded by the
Polynesian Cultural Center
Brigham Young University—Hawaii Campus

Published by The Institute for Polynesian Studies
Funded by the Polynesian Cultural Center
Brigham Young University—Hawaii Campus

Copyright © 1985 The Institute for Polynesian Studies

All Rights Reserved
Manufactured in the United States of America

ISBN 0-939154-38-2

Distributed for The Institute for Polynesian Studies
by the University of Hawaii Press:

Order Department
University of Hawaii Press
2840 Kolowalu Street
Honolulu, Hawaii 96822

Cover drawing by Martin Charlot
Monograph design by Pamela Kelley

No nā hoa 'imi loa ia buke me ke aloha

Acknowledgements

I would like to thank all those who helped me with this monograph, especially Samuel H. Elbert, Marshall Sahlins, Homer A. Hayes, and my students in the classes in which many of these ideas were first discussed. I want to thank also Colette Leimomi Akana for a suggestion, Leimomi Apoliona for information, and all the informants and friends named at various points in the monograph. Responsibility for all statements and mistakes rests, of course, with me. I thank also the Hawaiian Studies Program, University of Hawaii, for a grant for materials and The Institute for Polynesian Studies, more particularly Gloria Cronin and Judi Thompson, for accepting this monograph for publication in their series. For permission to use quotations, I thank the following publishers: The Bishop Museum Press, Honolulu; The University of Hawaii Press, Honolulu; Charles E. Tuttle Co., Inc., Tokyo, Japan; Associated Book Publishers, Auckland; and the Lili'uokalani Trust and the State Archives, State of Hawaii, for permission to quote Lili'uokalani 1897. References from Johnson 1975 and 1976 were checked with the original newspaper sources, from which all quotations and my translations were made.

Contents

INTRODUCTION	ix
1. Religion and Politics in Hawaiian Culture: The Place of Chiefs	1
2. Religio-Political Concepts in the Postcontact Period: The Kamehameha I Tradition	5
3. The Literature of the Kalākaua Dynasty	9
4. National Anthems	15
5. The Postmonarchy Period	24
6. A Politics of Beauty	29
APPENDIX 1 *The Use of* Akua *for Living Chiefs*	31
APPENDIX 2 *Uses of* Kapu *and* Kānāwai *in Hawaiian Literature*	37
APPENDIX 3 *The Hawaiian National Anthems and Related Texts*	41
E. O. Hall: *Restoration Anthem*	41
Announcement of the Contest for a National Anthem	43
Announcement of the Names of the Contest Judges	46
William Charles Lunalilo: *E Ola ka Mōʻī i ke Akua*	46
William Charles Lunalilo: *E Ola ka Mōʻī i ke Akua* (2)	47
Jno. I. Nāʻiliʻili: *Na ke Akua e Hoʻōla i ka Mōʻī!*	48
Peter K. Kaleikini: no title	49
J. P. Kānealiʻi: no title	50
Hawaiʻi: *He Mele no nā Liʻi*	51
Liliʻuokalani: *He Mele Lāhui Hawaiʻi*	52
He Himeni i haku ʻia no ka Mōʻī D. Kalākaua	53
Kalākaua: *Hawaiʻi Ponoʻī*	54

NOTES	55
GLOSSARY	77
BIBLIOGRAPHY	79

Introduction

The purpose of this monograph is to demonstrate the value of chants and songs as sources of information for the study of postcontact Hawaiian history. This is not intended as a complete survey of the available literature. Rather, I have restricted my attention to a small number of well-known examples, which can serve as an introduction to the field. Moreover, I will concentrate on a single aspect of political history: the role of chiefs and leaders.

Despite these restrictions, I must discuss a wide range of topics in history, religion, and literature. Many areas—such as genres, styles, and developments in Hawaiian literature—have not been studied sufficiently to allow of more than tentative conclusions. I have had to offer evidence, to give just one example, for the tendency of Hawaiian literature to stabilize or canonize a definite vocabulary within a literary form, even one recently introduced.

I have based my opinions almost exclusively on a study of primary Hawaiian-language sources, which I cite extensively. I have reluctantly decided to regularize the spelling and diacritical marks of certain texts quoted because of the existence of minor variants and/or typographical errors in those texts as published. I will note possibly controversial emendations. All translations are mine, and in a number of cases, I have retranslated titles. I refer to a work by its first line if no title has been provided. References in the notes are selective rather than comprehensive.

1.
Religion and Politics in Hawaiian Culture: The Place of Chiefs

The distinct Western categories of religion and politics cannot, of course, be imposed on Hawaiian culture. This is clear, for instance, from the fact that the American separation of church and state cannot be applied without distortion to the relations between *kāhuna* "priestly experts" and *ali'i* "chiefs." Those relations are characterized by a considerable amount of overlap and tension,[1] due most probably to a gradual, unsystematic separation of originally united functions.[2]

The chief is definitely a religious figure whose station is defined and supported by religious teachings. The principal doctrinal theory is that of a genealogy that links the chief to his illustrious, perhaps now deified ancestors; to the first humans; sometimes to the gods; and backwards in time through the animals, plants, and elements to the beginning of the universe.[3] A chief can, therefore, be discussed in cosmic terms. He is a *lani* "firmament." He descends from the sky-dwelling gods and from the male sky which mated with the female earth to begin the universal family line. His birth is a cosmic event.[4] Weather signs attend him. His death seems a cosmic disorder, a symptom of which is the breakdown of the social order during the mourning period.

The chief then is the link between the community, the gods, and the cosmos, and their mutual harmony depends on him. A good, right chief brings fertility and prosperity to his land. A bad, incorrect chief brings famine and drought. The fate of the people is linked to that of the chief.[5] In *Haui Ka Lani* "Fallen is the Chief," Ke'āulumoku chants of Kamehameha I:

He ali'i pono, he ali'i pono, he honua pono[6]

A right chief, a right chief, a right earth.

Later:

Akāka i kea ka pono o ka ʻāina
Hoʻokau ka pono o ke aliʻi[7]

The rightness of the land is clear to all.
The rightness of the chief has been founded.

Pono is a key word in Hawaiian politico-religious literature and has been defined very widely from moral righteousness to a correctness in practical terms that leads to success. In Hawaiian thinking, pono seems to incorporate both aspects: the right person must act rightly for the proper effect. A chanter needs both the correct family line and the proper training.

Accordingly, texts on chiefs can emphasize one or other aspect of pono. For instance, genealogical controversies stress inborn station. In *Haui Ka Lani*,

I hānau a pono ʻia mai ka mehameha[8]

The lonely one [Kamehameha] was born right.

The chant *Nahienaena* seems to be urging her marriage to her brother, a union that could produce high-ranking children. The word lani is used throughout for chief, evoking the primordial mating of sky with earth.

ʻO ka lani, kū[k]aʻi ka lani, mau ka honua
Kūkaʻi Kalani, mau ka honua iā Lani
Lani pipili, haʻamomoe leʻa
Pipili Kalani, mau ka honua ia[9]

The chief [firmament], the chief joins, the earth endures.
The Chief joins, the earth endures by/for the Chief
Clinging chiefs, laid down in delight.
The Chief clings, this earth endures.

No Keawenuiaumi "For Keawenuiaumi," mentions both station and action:

Ke aliʻi na e lana
E nānā ka ʻāina
Ka moku o kā lākou aliʻi pono
Pono no ka noho ʻana i ke aliʻi pono
He aliʻi no mai ka paʻa ke aliʻi
He kanaka ʻano ma i paʻa a ke kanaka[10]

That is the chief that planes above
Let the land look [at/to him]
The district of their right chief
Right indeed is the conduct of the right chief
[or: Right indeed is the way of life because of the right chief]
A chief indeed from the upper stratum is the chief
A human being of the type to associate himself firmly [to feel solidarity] with other men.

With the preservation of all due distinctions in functions and prerogatives, the relationship between chief and people should be controlled by the ideal of reciprocal *aloha* "love." The literature emphasizes at times the aloha of the chief for his people and at other times that of the people for their chief.[11]

Chiefly behavior can also be emphasized,[12] especially the ideal of religious piety.[13] Kekuaokalani is persuaded to resist Liholiho's abolition of the *kapu* "tabu" system with the argument

'O ka haipule ka mea kū i ka moku, akā, 'o nā li'i 'aiā,
  he 'ilihune.[14]

Piety is respected by the island, but irreligious chiefs
  are destitute.

The poetess Ululani praises the extent of Kamehameha I's religious observances, his nurturing support of the gods, in *A Chant of Welcome for Ka-mehameha:*

Ola ia kini akua iā 'oe[15]

These many gods live through you.

The above complex of ideas remains vital in Hawaiian politics through the monarchy period[16] and into the twentieth century. A further complex of ideas concerns the chief as family god. A ceremony could be performed at the death of a chief that would transform him into an *'aumakua* "family god." Calling a living high chief an *akua* "god," as a common practice at least, seems to be a late development—similar to one in the Roman imperial cult—from this earlier idea.[17] Certain of these ideas also were used with variations in the nineteenth century.[18]

Rivalries between chiefs were naturally reflected in literature. Legends could be recast by the ascendant group, or simply appropriated.

Genealogies could be redrawn.[19] Moreover, literature was a weapon to be used in such rivalries.[20] One could pray for and exalt one's chief. Genealogists would downgrade or question the lineage of rivals and substantiate that of their own chief.[21] Prophets and sorcerers would practice for their side.[22] Literature could be used to win adherents. Keʻāulumoku invites the islands:

Hele mai e noho i ka pono[23]

Come to dwell in the rightness.

All these elements can be found in later religio-political literature.

2.

Religio-Political Concepts in the Postcontact Period: The Kamehameha I Tradition

Postcontact culture in Hawai'i can be pictured as a spectrum with purely indigenous works at one extreme and purely imported ones at the other. Between those extremes can be found varying degrees of influence and synthesis.[24]

I have shown above that certain precontact ideas and practices continued into later Hawaiian politics. These came into contact with imported ideas, such as Christianity and democracy. Thus, for example, after the death of Kamehameha V, Lunalilo and later Kalākaua were elected king.

A most important idea for nineteenth-century politics forms, however, a distinct category: the tradition of Kamehameha I is an authentically indigenous response to a new age. That tradition has its source in the Kamehameha I rhetoric, the propaganda literature composed at various stages of Kamehameha's career. The earliest datable example of this is Ke'āulumoku's *Haui Ka Lani*, discussed above. Kamehameha is portrayed as pono in lineage and action, while his opponents are taunted and derided as inferiors and rebels.[25] Kamehameha is pious and a great warrior.[26] His reign will bring peace and prosperity. The poet prays for his long life and the well-being of all those around him.[27] These very same themes are repeated in the positive prose accounts of Kamehameha I and his career, which suggests a consciously created propaganda image.[28] This image was naturally disputed by his enemies, but became the standard view of Kamehameha I and his time and was later even further idealized.[29]

The general theme of the Kamehameha I tradition in later Hawaiian politics is that he is the nexus between precontact and postcontact Hawai'i, that he successfully met the challenge of the new age by uniting the islands and reforming Hawaiian culture—politics, religion, and society—so that it could be perpetuated. He solved the problems of contact, and his successors should follow the lines laid down by him.

This tradition of Kamehameha I assumed many forms. Kamehameha

I became the ancestral source of rank, closeness of kinship with him being used as the criterion in genealogical disputes.[30] At Kamehameha I's death, the ceremony was performed to transform him into an 'aumakua. Into the early missionary period, elaborate ceremonies were held on the anniversary of his death.[31] These ceremonies are evidence of an attempt to create a new, syncretistic religion from Hawaiian and non-Hawaiian sources to replace the traditional religion that had been abolished along with the kapu system shortly after Kamehameha's death.

Appeal was often made to Kamehameha I as an authority. In 1823 Kamāmalu, the wife of Kamehameha II, on leaving for England, chanted that they were following the command of Kamehameha I to take up the burden he had sought and for which he had suffered.[32] Kamehameha II stated, while engaged in manual labor: "Kamehameha's kingdom of work has come."[33] Kalākaua and Daggett correctly cited Kamehameha I's farming activities as a conscious model.[34] His alleged plan for an oceanic empire was used as a basis for an immigration policy and a direction in foreign affairs.[35] Kalākaua and his government presented themselves in general as extensions of the Kamehameha I tradition.[36]

The sayings of Kamehameha I have been taken as authoritative proverbs, mottos, and, at times, even as prophecies.[37] His *Māmalahoa Kānāwai* "The Law of the Broken Paddle" expresses the peacefulness and order he planned and later established over his domain:

E hele ka 'elemakule, ka luahine a me ke keiki
a moe i ke ala.

Let the old man, the old woman, and the child come
and sleep by the path.

This saying has often been cited as a realized or realizable ideal for the Hawaiian government.[38]

Before the battle of 'Īao, Maui, Kamehameha said to his warriors:

I mua, e nā pōki'i, a inu i ka wai 'awa'awa, 'a'ohe
hope e ho'i mai ai.

Forward, younger brothers, until you drink the bitter
water; there is no retreat into which to return.

This saying has been used in battle settings from the struggles at the accession of Kamehameha II at least until World War II.[39] In the current Hawaiian renaissance, Kalāhikiola Nali'i'elua, a religious teacher from Wai'anae, O'ahu, uses the saying as a prophecy of the conflicts

Religio-Political Concepts: The Kamehameha I Tradition 7

young Hawaiians will experience as they try to assert themselves politically. Another religious teacher joins the above saying with the ending of one by the priest and prophet Ka'ōpulupulu,⁴⁰ which he attributes to Kamehameha. To the *I mua* saying is added:

a pae i ke kai, no ka mea, no ke kai kā ho'i ka 'āina.

until you reach the sea, because to the sea indeed belongs the land.

This composite saying is interpreted as a prophecy of the gradual displacement of Hawaiians by Americans come from the sea.⁴¹

Most important for the Kamehameha I tradition were his last words, considered a testament:

E 'oni wale no 'oukou i ku'u pono a . . .⁴²

You need only act in my rightness and . . .

I have emphasized the importance of the word pono in Hawaiian religio-political literature. Kamehameha I is stating that he has laid down the right lines for his successors to follow. The pono of his own reign was later idealized.⁴³

These last words of Kamehameha I form the background, I would argue, for the famous statement of Kamehameha III on the restoration of Hawaiian sovereignty by England in 1843, a saying that has become the motto of the State of Hawaii:

Ua mau ke ea o ka 'āina i ka pono.

The life breath of the country has endured through rightness.

That is, he and his government had acted correctly in the crisis by pursuing a course of passive resistance and trust in the English government's eventual recognition of the justice of their position.⁴⁴ (Later, during the overthrow of the monarchy, Queen Lili'uokalani took this policy as her model, but her trust in the United States government was misplaced.) Kalākaua's premier, Walter Murray Gibson, quoted Kamehameha I's last words to inspire the people to nationalism.⁴⁵ Significantly, the missionaries and their adherents claimed that it was the pono of Christianity that preserved the country.⁴⁶

The Kamehameha tradition is expressed even in small details. For instance, Ernest K. Ka'ai's twentieth-century campaign song for Prince Kūhiō, *Kalaniana'ole*, pictures him saying:

Hōʻike ʻo Makoa kaʻu kūkini
My runner Makoa has made known . . .

The allusion is to a runner of Kamehameha I.⁴⁷

The Kamehameha I tradition could be used also as a standard by which to criticize an actual regime.⁴⁸ When one wished to act clearly counter to the tradition, some excuse had to be found.⁴⁹

3.
The Literature of the Kalākaua Dynasty

Kalākaua won the election to the throne only after a difficult campaign against Queen Emma, most of whose supporters remained loyal to her until her death. The non-Hawaiian community was also divided into factions, none of which were completely committed to Kalākaua. He had, therefore, to continue his campaign to win the support of the population, both for himself and for the dynasty he was establishing.[50] The members of that dynasty identified themselves with the nation,[51] so their efforts were directed to the broad goals of national identity and independence.

Literature was an important part of that movement and thus forms a parallel to Elizabethan works composed to affirm the controverted position of that queen. Kalākaua and his siblings—his sisters Lili'uokalani and Likelike, and his brother, Leleiōhoku—were great poets, descendants of the poet chiefess Ululani, and known collectively in the history of Hawaiian literature as *Nā Lani 'Ehā* "The Four Chiefs." Kalākaua also enlisted the aid of other poets, such as the Kaua'i chiefess J. Nahinu,[52] and generally revived Hawaiian chant and dance. Many of the works of this movement have become classics and form a strong influence on current conceptions of Hawaiian literature.

The frequent recurrence of certain themes, terms, and patterns suggests that much of the Kalākaua literature is the result of conscious decision and concerted effort. *Kawika*—a short, popular hula name chant for Kalākaua[53]—contains those themes *in nuce:* heights, rank, shining, fame in distant lands, and the chief as flower. Kalākaua is *ka heke a'o nā pua* "the highest of the flowers" (l. 2); *ka pua i luna* "the flower above" (l. 7). Like lightning from the east, he illumes, *mālamalama*, Hawai'i (ll. 3f.). He is known in foreign lands like Britain and France (ll. 5f.). His lineage is distinguished (l. 8). He is a chief (l. 10).

The same combination of themes can be found in other Kalākaua chants. In Nahinu's *Iā 'Oe e Ka Lā e 'Alohi Nei* "For You, O Glittering Sun," composed on Kalākaua's trip around the world,[54] there are constant references to heights, which symbolize his rank (ll. 2, 4, 6f., 9ff.). The theme of shining is derived from Kalākaua's name, "The Day or Sun of Battle" (ll. 1, 4).[55] The chief's fame in foreign lands is the main theme of the chant and is connected to the theme of heights by line 12:

> Nāna i hehei ia kapu o Kahiki
>
> His it is to trample on the tabus of distant lands.[56]

Although Kalākaua is not called a *pua* "flower" in the chant, his personal beauty and sexuality, expressed by that theme, are emphasized (ll. 3, 7–10).[57]

Another name chant, 'O *Kalākaua, he inoa*,[58] emphasizes his designation as pua (ll. 2f., 11) and links it both to one of his private names—Kapuamae'oleikalā "The Flower that Wilts Not in the Sun"—and, as in *Kawika*, to the theme of heights (ll. 3–8):

> Ke pua mai la i ka mauna
>
> He flowers forth there on the mountain.

The theme of shining is also present (ll. 5, 6 *Mālamalama*, 9f.)[59]; it is expressed in lines 5 and 9 as burning, which connects it with the volcano region, the locus of the chant, and the volcanic Pele religion.[60] Fame in foreign lands is not mentioned, in all likelihood because this chant is based on classical models.

These themes can all, of course, be found in earlier literature and singly in contemporary and later works. However, their regular, conjoined use—along with other themes—establishes them as elements of a formal rhetoric. Moreover, they express key points of Kalākaua's views and policies: heights and shining express his high rank; foreign fame, the place he wished to establish for Hawai'i in the world community; and the pua theme, the regeneration of his race.

These themes could be linked to others. David Malo's *He Inoa Ahi nō Kalākaua* "A Fire Name Chant for Kalākaua," shows how the theme of shining or burning could have a very precise reference and use in the Kalākaua movement.[61] The import of the chant can be understood in the context of Hawaiian uses of kapu and *kānāwai* "law." A tabu or law could have a name, a fixed formulation similar to a proverb, and a story of its origin, which included the name of the important chief involved in its foundation. Non-godly kapu and kānāwai were usually connected to chiefs, could be inherited or won, and were points of prestige to be mentioned in chants praising a chief.[62]

Malo's chant of praise is based on a prestigious kapu inherited by

Kalākaua: the privilege of burning torches by day. The mention of that kapu privilege evokes Kalākaua's high and ancient lineage and his connection to Kamehameha I. Kapu privilege is, in fact, another theme of the Kalākaua movement.[63] Moreover, this kapu was the basis for ceremonies that combined traditional Hawaiian elements with foreign ones, such as fireworks and torchlight parades then used in U.S. political campaigns. That is, religio-political traditions, literature, and ceremonies were being used conjointly to support Kalākaua's position.

The chants discussed above have the traditional function of praising the chief and to this end use largely traditional ideas. But their literary structures and devices vary from the traditional to more modern. Malo's chant, despite the modernity of many of the objects mentioned in it, is most traditional in form. The ceremonial fires set in different places are listed and characterized in order of their appearance before the passengers traveling on a boat between Makapu'u and Honolulu harbor. Each line contains a complete thought. The length of the lines varies according to the requirements of their contents. The chants *Iā 'Oe e Ka Lā* and *'O Kalākaua, he inoa* are shorter, more regular and tightly organized, and contain run-on lines, generally more recent developments, I would argue, in Hawaiian poetry.

Another characteristic is the emphatic personal tone, perceptible in *Iā 'Oe e Ka Lā* in the frequent references to the chief's beauty. In much of the poetry of the Kalākaua dynasty, stylistic combinations are made of public chants—traditionally heroic and less personal—and private songs of affection. For instance, private family names are regularly used in poetry intended to be public. The purpose of this mixing of genres, which can be found in other areas of nineteenth-century Hawaiian literature as well, was apparently to inspire a devotion to the chief as a person. That is, an attempt was being made to strengthen the traditional relationship of reciprocal aloha between chief and subject by introducing an element of devoted affection arising from a sense of familiarity with the person and, to some extent, the private life and feelings of the chief. This parallels the public presentation of Queen Victoria in her domestic role as wife and mother and later widow, a presentation that had been closely followed by Queen Emma in the photographs taken of her mourning her husband and child.[64]

In the last stanza of *E Nihi Ka Hele* "Tread Softly," by the Healani Glee Club on the occasion of Queen Kapi'olani's departure for England in 1887,[65] the languages of government and love poetry are curiously joined:

E hele me ka poina 'ole
E huli 'ē ke alo i hope nei.

Eia kō lei kalaunu,
'O ka 'ōnohi o Hawai'i.

Go without forgetfulness.
Turn your face again to those you have left behind you here.
Here is your crown *lei,*
The center of Hawai'i.

The first two lines could be taken from a love poem. The last two are definitely governmental. Similarly, in line 8 of Lili'uokalani's *He Inoa Nō Ka'iulani*[66] "A Name Chant for Ka'iulani," she calls her niece:

Pua ha'aheo o ke aupuni

Cherished flower of the government.

This mixing of genres demonstrates also that the Kalākaua siblings identified themselves with their stations. For instance, in stanza 2 of Lili'uokalani's moving *He Kanikau No Lele-iō-hoku*[67] "A Dirge for Lele-iō-hoku," Kalākaua is called by his private family name and depicted wailing (ll. 3f.):

" 'Auhea ku'u pōki'i,
Ka ho'oilina aupuni?"

"Where is my little brother,
The successor to the government?"

The need to express new content could prompt the creation of new literary forms. In *Ka Momi*[68] "The Pearl," Kalākaua shares his innermost reflections, even his thought processes, with his people after returning from his world tour in 1881: although his kingdom is smaller than those of the monarchs he met, he can boast that—unlike other rulers, who must fear assassination[69]—he enjoys *ke aloha pili pa'a* "the close affection" (l. 18) of his people. This introspective, public communication is unprecedented, as far as I can see, in Hawaiian literature. Kalākaua does not present himself on the heights, but humbled by his encounter with the world powers, even dependent for moral support on his people. Moreover, he has received, rather than earned, the aloha of his people as "a pearl sent down from above," an uncharacteristic Christian tinge possibly inspired by the mood of the occasion of the chant.

Although *Ka Momi* is a chant, the language employed is close to prose: syntactical structures are usually given in full, not compressed or eliminated; there are no allusions or ambiguous uses of words to create several levels of meaning.

The esthetic effect of *Ka Momi* is also close to that of Hawaiian prose. Poetry was traditionally a proper occasion for brilliance and the display of learning, as apparently were also certain prose genres such as funeral or mourning oratory.[70] But most traditional prose writers strive for exactness and concision of expression, understatement, and simplicity, qualities with which the best authors create a distinctive elegance.[71] The esthetic achievement of *Ka Momi* is to realize those qualities so successfully that they stimulate a sense of elevation worthy of the chant form in which they are being used so innovatively to communicate a hitherto unexpressed dimension of the relationship between chief and people.

Kalākaua's *Ke Aliʻi Milimili*[72] "The Beloved Chief," 1890, is equally innovative. The purpose of the chant—to proclaim the regency of Liliʻuokalani during the king's absence—has no parallel in Hawaiian literature, as far as I can see. The tone is more public and formal, as befits a proclamation, and use is made of traditional expressions.[73] On the other hand, the element of personal devotionalism noted earlier is expressed in the use of private family names (ll. 12, 20), and especially *milimili* "cherished or fondled one" (title and l. 14).[74] Liliʻuokalani is both Hawaiʻi's aliʻi and milimili, another expression of the reciprocal aloha between chief and people. Similarly, Liliʻuokalani is the one who is believed, *hilinaʻi*, and beloved, *aloha*, by the people (ll. 17f).

The islands are called upon in traditional fashion to see, *ʻike*, the crown flag waving high despite all troubles. That flag is for Liliʻuokalani,[75] the successor to the crown. Kalākaua shows her to Hawaiʻi; *Nānā ʻia*, "she is looked at" (l. 13). Then he addresses her directly: until he returns (ll. 21f.):

ʻO kou aupuni.
E ka lani, nānā ʻia.

It is your government.
Oh chief, look to it.

By playing on the phrase *nānā ʻia*, passive in line 13 and imperative in line 22, Kalākaua has expressed his theory of government: the people look to the chief,[76] and the chief looks to the government. The relationship of aloha is structured by distinct, but connected and complementary responsibilities. Significantly, Liliʻuokalani restated this view in a speech made during the crisis that led to her overthrow:

e hoomau i ka nana mai Ia'u, a pela hoi Au e nana aku ai ia
oukou. E hoopaa Ia'u iloko o ko oukou aloha.[77]

persevere in looking to me, as I also will look out for you. Make
me firm in your aloha/Make for me a solid place within your
affection.

4.
National Anthems

The Hawaiian national anthems are prime examples of bicultural religio-political thinking and expression (see Appendix 3).
The national anthem is a clear example of an introduced literary form.[78] The model adopted in Hawai'i was *God Save the King*. The poetry is thus in the form of Western lyrics: regular and adapted to Western melody. Moreover, the concepts expressed by that model—most obviously, a Christian theory of kingship—influenced the views expressed in the Hawaiian anthems.[79]

An anthem also entails the idea of a unity and loyalty broader than the more traditional local or dynastic ones. The creation and inculcation of that idea was in fact a constant task for the monarchy established by Kamehameha I's conquests, the ideological parallel to governmental reorganization.[80]

Included in the creation of an idea of a unified nation was that of a viable picture of Hawaiian society. As in other areas of nineteenth-century Hawaiian culture, the method used was the selection of certain elements of traditional culture for perpetuation, a process that resulted in a general simplification of the picture of the society. For instance, in the anthems, the nobles are not described in all the traditional complexity of their rankings, but as a single order (out of four in Lili'uokalani's anthem, or out of three in Kalākaua's). The Hawaiian anthems are, therefore, important expressions of the development of Hawaiian political thinking and expression.

Edwin O. Hall's popular *Restoration Anthem* of 1843 apparently served as an unofficial anthem and influenced later compositions, notably those by Lunalilo and Kaleikini, and *He Himeni*. Hall also served on the jury that selected Lunalilo's anthem as the winner of the contest sponsored by *Ka Nupepa Kuokoa* in 1861–1862. Hall's verse, based loosely on *God Save the King*, honors "our rightful king" in its first stanza; "the worthy name" of Admiral Thomas, restorer of Hawaiian sovereignty, in the second stanza; and "our Heavenly King," in the third. No use is made of Hawaiian symbols, poetic devices, or concepts. The anthem is, therefore, despite its use of the Hawaiian language, purely Western and Christian in conception.

The *Kuokoa* contest was announced by the newspaper's editor, Henry M. Whitney, on 16 December 1861. The names of the judges, all non-Hawaiians, were published on 25 January 1862, and Lunalilo's winning entry was printed on 8 February. Other compositions prompted by the contest were published in later issues.

Contest rule 5 insisted that the entries adhere closely to the form of *God Save the King:* they should contain only four stanzas and fit the melody of the British anthem. The importance of this rule is shown by the judges' complaint in announcing the winner that the majority of the entries had not followed the melody exactly.

Contest rule 6 insisted further that entries conform closely to the 'ano "character, sense" of the British anthem. In aid of this, that anthem was printed in English with a prose paraphrase in Hawaiian. Stanza 3, which refers to the prince, was localized in the paraphrase by using the phrase *ka Haku o Hawaii*, the title of the reigning monarch's son.

The losing compositions follow closely, even slavishly, the contest rules and the paraphrase. The first stanza refers to the king; the second, to the queen; the third, to the prince; and the last, to all three. The Christian theocentric view of kingship is unadulterated, and there are only a few, merely incidental uses of Hawaiian concepts.

Lunalilo's winning anthem is clearly influenced by Hall's *Restoration Anthem* and the *Kuokoa* paraphrase in both form and vocabulary.[81] However, while the compositions of Lunalilo's predecessor and competitors are mere verse, his attains the level of true poetry.

Lunalilo accomplishes this by several means. He gains a certain freedom of movement by adhering less closely to the proffered models. He expresses himself more often in symbols and images from both Hawaiian and Western literature, rather than baldly stating his points.

He also uses the important Hawaiian poetic device of ambiguity. His anthem can in fact be read in two different ways. He could be following the contest model and dedicating the first three stanzas individually to king, queen, and prince, and the last to all three. In that case, *lākou* (st. 4, l. 6) would refer in recapitulation to those three, as it does in the *Kuokoa* paraphrase and the compositions of Nāʻiliʻili and Kāneali'i. The anthem can, however, be interpreted as referring throughout to the king. The king alone is explicitly designated (st. 1, l. 3). Possible references to queen and prince—so unambiguous in the paraphrase and the other compositions—are made in symbols that are equally appropriate to the king. As a result, in Lunalilo's second version of the anthem, written on his accession to the throne, he could appropriate the images of stanza 2 to himself (those of the third stanza are dropped). This concentration on the ruler is, in my opinion, a Hawaiianization of the British anthem's interest in the royal family. The anthem more nearly resembles the traditional form of the *mele inoa*, a chant in praise of a single person or chief. The lākou of stanza 4 would then have a broader reference to all the people of the government (such as the chiefs mentioned in line 2) or even to the people of the nation.

Lunalilo's composition established the anthem as a truly Hawaiian poetic form and strongly influenced subsequent ones.[82] He also introduced important traditional Hawaiian concepts as major components of the anthem's meaning. The tension between those traditional concepts and the Christian ones received from the foreign model was expressive of the intellectual climate of the times and continued as a basic problem through the later anthems.

On the one hand, the anthem expresses a theocentric Christian idea of kingship in which life, blessings, power, and protection are given by the Christian God, the King of Kings.[83] This view is implicit in the very title of the anthem, *E Ola ka Mōʻī i ke Akua* "May the King Live through God." The anthem is in fact a prayer to God to aid king and country.

On the other hand, Lunalilo uses several phrases that express traditional Hawaiian views of chiefs, according to which chiefs possess certain positive qualities of their own. The Hawaiian character of these concepts remains the same whether they are applied to king, queen, or prince.

Stanza 2 (l. 2) of *God Save the King* speaks of "a gentler name," that of the queen. The *Kuokoa* paraphrases this as *he inoa hou* "a new name." That is, the name is now being mentioned as a new subject for praise. Hall (st. 2, l. 1) adapted *God Save the King* to the occasion with *ka inoa maikaʻi* "the good name" of Admiral Thomas. In sharp contrast, Lunalilo's phrase (st. 2, l. 1), *Ka inoa kamahaʻo* "the wondrous name" (of the king or queen), evokes specific Hawaiian ideas of the importance of names, especially those of chiefs,[84] and describes the name as *kamahaʻo*, a word used for objects that stimulate a sense of religious awe.[85] Significantly, the phrase is made to apply to Lunalilo's own name in his second version of the anthem. That name, which is an infinite superlative of "above," was indicative of Lunalilo's exalted lineage.

Lei nani "beautiful lei" (st. 2, l. 2) and *ka pua nani* "the beautiful flower" (st. 3, l. 6) express the chief's physical attractiveness and fertility.

Most important is the reference (st. 3, l. 3) to the king or the prince as the *pōkiʻi* "younger brother" of God.[86] This statement could evoke in the minds of some listeners the traditional idea of the chief's descent from the gods.[87] A nearer interpretation, I would argue, is that the word has been taken from a famous saying of Kamehameha I.[88] That is, Lunalilo is placing the anthem in the Kamehameha I tradition, as can be seen also in the reference to the Kamehameha III saying in stanza 4 (ll. 4f.).[89] Kamehameha I's designation of his warriors as his pōkiʻi could be taken literally,[90] but seems to have become a conventional reference for the nobles under the king.[91] This relationship is being used now by Lunalilo to describe that between the king and God.

Significantly, the amended version of Lunalilo's anthem used on his accession to the throne places more emphasis on the king's role. The second of three stanzas is devoted entirely to him. He is the lei nani (l. 4); his is the *inoa kamahaʻo*, Lunalilo (ll. 1f.); and he is asked to turn with aloha toward his people. The first and second stanzas are theocentric and addressed to God.

In both versions of his anthem, Lunalilo expresses a view that is a combination, rather than a synthesis, of theocentric Christianity and the traditional Hawaiian view that the king has positive qualities of his own. He expresses this view also in his letter accepting the contest prize: he hopes to compose better works in the future, *ke kokua pu mai ke Akua i kaʻu hana* "if God seconds me in my work."[92] The same view is again expressed in Lunalilo's accession speech:

> E nana alohaia mai kakou e ka Makua Nui o ka Lani, no ka mea, ina i nele i Kona Kokua, alaila, ua makehewa ko kakou hooikaika ana e hapai i na pono o ke Aupuni a me ka Lahui.[93]
>
> May we be looked on with aloha by the Great Father of Heaven, because, if His Help is lacking, our efforts to support the rights of the Government and People/Race will be in vain.

The main thrust of Liliʻuokalani's anthem, *He Mele Lāhui Hawaiʻi*, is to emphasize and extend the theocentric Christianity already present in Lunalilo's. Even more than in his anthem, the dominant tone is one of prayer.[94] We approach with *naʻau haʻahaʻa* "lowly insides" (st. 1, l. 4) and beg for God to turn toward us (st. 1, ll. 2f.), appealing to his *ahonui* "patience" (st. 2, l. 7; st. 3, l. 6), and so on. That all power comes from God is stressed repeatedly. He establishes peace (st. 1, ll. 5–8). He protects the king and keeps him on his throne (st. 2, ll. 1–4). He guards the people (st. 3, l. 5) and gives life to them and the king (chorus, ll. 3f.; st. 2, ll. 7f.). The word for life, *ola*, recurs in conjunction with *mau* "enduring," evoking the Christian idea of *ola mau* "eternal life."

Liliʻuokalani has accepted the Christian themes from Lunalilo's anthem but not the offsetting Hawaiian ones.[95] On the contrary, she expressly Christianizes the Kamehameha III saying (chorus, ll. 1f.): the life of the land endures in *God's* pono.[96] The king is not accorded any intrinsic value. Even his inner qualities are given by God, as in stanza 2 (ll. 5f.) when God is asked to place aloha into the king's *naʻau* "insides."[97] In the Christianity expressed by Liliʻuokalani in this anthem, all good comes from God alone; the king is at best a conduit. Similarly, she emphasizes virtues favored by Christians: peace, humility, and patience.

Liliʻuokalani goes beyond Lunalilo in her interest in formulating a picture of the nation's society. Lunalilo referred simply to God, the king, and "us" or "they" (the second version used *lāhui* "race or people"). Liliʻuokalani emphasizes unity by using traditional phrases referring to Hawaiʻi as a whole (st. 1, ll. 6f.). She articulates a picture of society organized into four orders or ranks: the king (chorus, l. 4; st. 2), the chiefs (st. 3, l. 2), the *makaʻāinana* "people of the land" (st. 3, l. 3), and the *lehulehu* "multitude" (st. 3, l. 4), which I take to be the rest of the population, most likely non-Hawaiian.[98] Of these orders, the king receives the most emphasis. The chiefs are "of the Government" and "with the people of the land." That is, Hawaiian society is a unity organized in connected but descending ranks under God, from whom are derived the virtues necessary for well-being.

Liliʻuokalani's anthem became a second basis, along with Lunalilo's, for the next two anthems:[99] the first, *He Himeni*, is an anonymous example of the Kalākaua propaganda literature; the second, *Hawaiʻi Ponoʻī*, is by Kalākaua himself. Despite their dependence on previous anthems, both differ strikingly from them. In *He Himeni*, the Christian element has been reduced to stanza 3 (ll. 1ff.): "we" are described as praying to God for Kalākaua's life, which is clearly described (l. 4) as *kou ola nei* "your life here" rather than as the Christian ola mau, which does not appear at all in the anthem.[100] This reference to Christianity seems to be one of those "grace notes" with which Hawaiians reassure non-Hawaiian listeners when they are speaking of Hawaiian matters in a Hawaiian way.

On the other hand, the traditional Hawaiian views have been emphasized and extended. Kalākaua himself, rather than God, is addressed in the first line (God appears only much later in the anthem). What was given by God in the previous anthems is now given by Kalākaua. In Lunalilo's anthem (st. 1, l. 2) God is asked to give *pōmaikaʻi* "well-being"; in *He Himeni* (st. 1, l. 3) Kalākaua is asked to give it along with his *kōkua* "aid" (l. 2). In Lunalilo's anthem (st. 2, l. 5) God is asked to *pale na ʻino e* "ward off ills," while in *He Himeni* (st. 2, l. 5) *ua pau nā ʻino e* "the ills are over" with Kalākaua's accession to the throne.[101] In Liliʻuokalani's anthem (st. 1, ll. 5–8) the country is unified in peace under God's *malu*, the undisturbed shelter of his kapu; in *He Himeni* (st. 1, ll. 4–7) the new king, Kalākaua himself, unites the nation. In his later chant *Ka Momi* (l. 10) Kalākaua writes that Hawai'i's population is *malalo o ko'u malu* "in the shelter of my kapu" or "in the realm of my authority."[102]

He Himeni is clearly abandoning the theocentric view that all good comes from God and returning to a traditional Hawaiian view of the chief. The anthem resembles not a Christian prayer but a chant in praise of a chief. Kalākaua's victory in the election is described as a conquest that resembles those of Kamehameha I: he unites the islands to establish order. This warrior theme—standard in the Kalākaua literature—is the direct opposite of Lili'uokalani's emphasis on Christian peace. All these characteristics identify *He Himeni* as an example of the Kalākaua propaganda literature.[103]

He Himeni seems also to be narrowing the picture of Hawaiian society. In stanza 3 (ll. 4ff.) the king is to live with all the chiefs and the maka'āinana; that is, the author omits the lehulehu, the undifferentiated multitude mentioned by Lili'uokalani. The nobles and the people of the land would normally be Hawaiian, although some non-Hawaiians were ennobled. The author seems to be expressing in a covert way the Kalākaua racialist policy, later to be expressed by the slogan "Hawai'i for Hawaiians."

The themes of national unity and social organization become the main structural principles of Kalākaua's own anthem. That anthem is addressed to *Hawai'i pono'ī* "Hawaii's own," a phrase that is a stroke of poetic genius, suggesting, as a singular, the unity of the nation as well as its problems: there are those who truly belong to Hawai'i and those who do not. Pono'ī is a composite of pono—in the sense of what is one's rightful property, truly one's own—and 'ī, an archaic intensifier. The theme of national unity—patriotism and loyalty—is brought to the forefront of the anthem.

Each of the three stanzas is devoted to a social order, which it characterizes: the first to the king,[104] the second to the nobles,[105] and the third to the lāhui.[106] This reproduces the tripartite scheme of the first anthem. As is traditional in Hawaiian anthems, more lines are devoted to the king than to the other orders (st. 1; chorus). The king is referred to repeatedly in traditional, honorific terms, lani and ali'i, which evoke the Kalākaua theme of heights and rank. This is in line with *He Himeni* (st. 2, ll. 6f.):

Ua kau ka lei ali'i,
Maluna ou.

The noble *lei* [the crown] has been placed
On you.

The warrior imagery of *He Himeni* is continued in *Hawai'i Pono'ī:* the kingdom is defended *me ka ihe* "with the spear" (chorus, l. 4).[107]

In *He Himeni*, a vague similitude was noted between Kalākaua's election victory and the career of Kamehameha I. In the chorus of *Hawai'i Pono'ī*, a very explicit link is claimed between the two monarchs, which makes the passage a key expression of the Kamehameha I tradition.

The first line of the chorus is ambiguous: *Makua lani e* could be addressing the Heavenly Father, the Christian God. In fact, this use is common in Hawaiian Christian prayers and political rhetoric,[108] and most Hawaiians so understand the line today. The same words could also be translated "chiefly father," lani being understood as a proverbial reference to the origin of chiefs in the firmament. That this second interpretation is correct is clear from the parallel line 2, which addresses Kamehameha. That the lines refer to only one person—and not to both God and Kamehameha—can be argued from line 3, in which the dual, inclusive, second-person pronoun *kāua* "we two" is used: the speaker and the *one* person addressed. Moreover, the designation of Kamehameha as *makua* "father" can be found in Ke'āulumoku's *Haui Ka Lani*, a basic work of the Kamehameha I rhetoric.[109] Such ambiguities are not accidental in Hawaiian literature. Kalākaua seems to be creating a Christian grace note without really introducing a Christian element into the anthem.

Kamehameha I is, therefore, the makua, the head of the genealogy. This same use of makua—to designate that member of a long genealogy whom one wishes to emphasize and take as a basis for the claim one is making—can be found in other chants. In *Kawika* (l. 8) Kalākaua's father, Kapa'akea, is named as the makua, and in *He Lei no Ka'iulani* (l. 27) Kalākaua himself is named as the founder of the kingly dynasty to the rights of which Ka'iulani lays claim.[110]

Kamehameha I is also an abiding presence who can be addressed and comes to aid.[111] In lines 3–4 of the chorus,

Na kāua e pale
Me ka ihe.

It is for us two to fend off
With the spear.

Kamehameha I is obviously one of the two mentioned. The second can only be Kalākaua himself. He is the speaker just as he is in his *Ka Momi* and *Ke Ali'i Milimili*. In both those chants he addresses his people, as he does in *Hawai'i Pono'ī*. In *Ke Ali'i Milimili* and *Hawai'i Pono'ī* he addresses a second person as well: respectively, Lili'uokalani and Kamehameha I. The three poems are thus united in style and thought.

Kalākaua is, therefore, uniting himself with Kamehameha I—the lani ali'i with the makua lani—to defend, as warriors, the kingdom. This position is in accord with *He Himeni*, in which the king is active, and is opposed to that of the previous anthems, which prayed for the Christian God to protect the nation.[112] Kalākaua's activism is given a foundation in the Kamehameha I tradition. The nobles also are described in terms of that tradition, which defines their place as under Kamehameha's successor as monarch.[113]

The role of the lāhui is to *ui*—a word that has been translated very divergently.[114] The primary dictionary meaning—"To ask, question, appeal, turn to for help or advice, query"[115]—yields the best sense: the people should turn to their hereditary rulers for guidance. This is the point of asking Hawai'i pono'ī to *nānā* "look" to the king and the nobles, just as in *Ke Ali'i Milimili* Hawai'i should look to Lili'uokalani while she looks to the government. The same word, nānā, is used in both poems.[116]

The structure of society is expressed by the descriptions of its three orders and also by the sequence in which they are presented. All look up to the king. The lowest order—the fulfillment of whose duties is an honorable *hana nui* "great work"—looks up also to the nobles. The unity of the society is seen also in the fact that the king belongs to Hawai'i pono'ī: "your king" (st. 1, l. 2).[117] The dependence of the king on his people was also a theme of *Ka Momi*.

Hawai'i Pono'ī expresses important themes of Kalākaua's thought and policy: a unified nation structured in descending ranks; an activist king in the Kamehameha I tradition; a racial emphasis. These themes are expressed with great concision and discretion, in marked contrast to *He Himeni*.

Also discreet is the religious but non-Christian character of the anthem. All references to the Christian God are omitted, as are words like pōmaika'i and ola which were closely connected to Christianity in previous anthems. As a result, *Hawai'i Pono'ī* seems completely nonreligious and entirely political. The politics of the anthem are, however, Hawaiian: based on traditional views of chiefs that cannot be separated from the indigenous religion. The original title of the anthem, *Hymn of Kamehameha I*, must be taken seriously.

Hawaiʻi Ponoʻī, like so many postcontact works, seems designed to exploit the gap between Hawaiian and non-Hawaiian understanding. Such obfuscation is traditionally considered a skill in Polynesian literature and was one which—along with poetic genius and reflection—enabled Kalākaua to create the first truly original Hawaiian anthem.

5.
The Postmonarchy Period

Religio-political chants and songs of the postmonarchy period clearly base themselves on the vocabulary[118] and themes[119] established earlier, with additions that reflect the new circumstances.[120]

    The chant *He Lei no Ka'iulani* pictures her asking for the return of her *kuleana* "responsibility" to be sovereign (ll. 9f., 15f., 23ff., 33f.). This demand is equated in the chant with that for the *ea* and *ola* "life" of Hawai'i (ll. 6, 13f., 20), an allusion to the saying of Kamehameha III and the view that the right chief is necessary for the well-being of the community and the cosmos. That she is the right chief is claimed in the proclamation of her rank. Lines 4, 16, and 28 express the Kalākaua dynasty theme of kapu, specifically the *wohi kapu*,[121] a sign of high rank that, in line 16, is described as sacred. Ka'iulani's rank, and thus her kuleana, are founded genealogically *mai ka pō mai* "from out of the night" (l. 25), a traditional expression for the distant past, which has religious connotations.[122] Significantly, Kalākaua is now named as the makua of the genealogy (ll. 26f.), just as Kamehameha I was in *Hawai'i Pono'ī*. That is, the Kalākaua dynasty is finding its genealogical foundation and authority in its founder, rather than in its relationship to Kamehameha I. The continuing influence of the Kamehameha I tradition can, however, be found in the statement that Kalākaua sought, *'imi* (l. 26), the kuleana of sovereignty, just as Kamehameha I was pictured as having done in the chant of Kamāmalu.[123]

    To this genealogical foundation (as in l. 30), the chant adds a second basis for Ka'iulani's station: the lāhui (ll. 4, 29). She is the child not only of her ancestors but of the race as a whole. Moreover, she appeals to that race for justification (ll. 22ff.). This theme of the dependence of the chief or leader on the people, expressed earlier in *Ka Momi*, for example, becomes increasingly prominent—at first, to rally the people behind the monarchy, as in *Kaulana Nā Pua*,[124] and later, to win elections.

    The chant is typical of those Kalākaua dynasty works that add to the public or official mode an expression of personal feeling[125] (l. 31):

Māpu ke aloha i ka puʻuwai
Aloha surges up in the heart.

The use of *puʻuwai* "heart" as the seat of the emotions is a Westernism found in Biblical literature and love songs,[126] which began to be used increasingly in political poetry.[127] Characteristically for the literature of the time, a traditional, even archaic, expression of emotion follows in line 32:

Hana mau ana hoʻi i ka iwihilo
Working constantly in the thighbone.

Genealogical thinking entails a multidimensional appreciation of and emphasis on the body. There is no trace of Christianity in the chant.

Kalanianaʻole, a campaign song of remarkably noble tone and high poetic quality, absorbs an astonishing number of traditional elements into an esthetic unity.[128] Although the campaign is for delegate to the United States Congress, the candidate is presented as a royal chief[129] proclaimed by traditional weather signs (ll. 13f.). However, just as in the previous chant, his dependence on the people is expressed. The islands are called on in the traditional way for kōkua (l. 26; in *He Himeni* it was the king who gave kōkua to the people, st. 1, l. 2). Just as Kaʻiulani in *He Lei no Kaʻiulani* (l. 4) was called

ʻO ka wohi kūkahi o ka lāhui
The outstanding wohi chief of the race

so Kūhiō is (l. 22)

Ka wohi a ka lāhui
The wohi chief of [or by] the race.

The wish for him is uttered (l. 27):

E ola ʻoe me kou lāhui
May you live with your race.

In the style of the Kalākaua dynasty, words expressive of private affections are used to inculcate a sense of personal devotion to the candidate.[130] Just as in the previous chant, there is no reference to Christianity. On the contrary, the song is clearly based on traditional Hawaiian religion in its concept of the chief, mention of weather signs or omens (ll. 13f.), address to gods (l. 21), and possible reference to sorcery.[131]

Lanakila Iaukea also perpetuates the chiefly ideology within the democratic process.[132] The candidate's genealogically founded rank is stressed (st. 2, ll. 1ff.). The image of heights is used to express his position in his elective office (st. 1, l. 3; chorus, l. 3). Again, there is no reference whatsoever to Christianity.[133]

He Wehi A He Lei No Kalama uses traditional elements—for instance, heights imagery for elective office (ll. 5f., 8)—but is decidedly nonaristocratic. Kalama is *ka moho a ka lāhui* "the candidate of the race/people" (l. 2). His station is based not on genealogical rank but on the fact that (l. 3)

Ua koho pono 'ia

He has been rightly elected.

The song boasts unabashedly of victory and lords it over the defeated (ll. 7–14). Points alluded to poetically elsewhere are here made explicit. The sexual connotation of the reference to the chief as pua is turned into a taunt (l. 14):

'A'ohe huapala e loa'a mai

No ripe fruit [lover] will be obtained [by his enemies].

The allusion to weather signs and omens in *Kalaniana'ole* (ll. 13f.) is explicitly related to "kahunaism," the reading of signs in the sky by sorcerers. The kahuna of the opposing side was *pa'a* "bound" by the *mana* of Kalama's ancestors and by the mana of the Trinity (ll. 19f.), a yoking together of traditional Hawaiian religion and Christianity.[134] Curiously, although the song is nonaristocratic, it is an almost unbroken paean to Kalama, with just passing reference to his dependence on the people. As such, the song is paradoxically nearer to earlier chants in praise of chiefs than those aristocratic works that stress dependence on the people.

Kamuela King absorbs into a seamless simplicity the various elements that had become traditional to the genre of campaign songs.[135] The Hawaiian ideology of chiefs, an appeal to emotions, a dominant but not oppressive Christian theology, and representative democracy are each evoked with a small selection of terms that had all, by the time of composition, become traditional.[136] This irenic combination of ideas recalls Lunalilo's *E Ola ka Mō'ī i ke Akua*, but *Kamuela King* is more convincing because of its perfect smoothness, the result perhaps of generations of removing the rough edges from mutually incompatible ideas.

The literary form of the campaign song was developed over several generations and apparently never became completely independent of the forms on which it was based.[137] The protest song seems, however, to have been created with one work. Although it uses traditional elements,[138] Ellen Wright Prendergast's *Kaulana Nā Pua* "Famous Are the Flowers" has no real precedent as far as I can see. It differs from earlier works, such as *Haui Ka Lani*, in a number of ways. *Kaulana Nā Pua* is definitely a song, that is, a Hawaiian adaptation of a Western form. The situation is a civil rather than a battle contest. The song protests verbally against past and possible future actions and uses moral suasion and the weight of public opinion rather than threats of physical violence.

Most important, the dispute is described not as intracultural—between chiefs—but intercultural, between Hawaiian and Western culture. The '*enemi* "enemy" (st. 3, l. 2) is described as having *loko 'ino* "evil insides" (st. 1, l. 3). Rather than oral, face-to-face communication, he uses written documents, *pepa* (st. 3, l. 2), and *palapala* (st. 1, l. 4), a word still used bitterly by some Hawaiians to describe the rules established by an alien culture to favor its own members.[139] The palapala is '*ānunu* "greedy" (st. 1, l. 4), considered a serious vice in a society based on generous hospitality.[140] Western culture is depicted as basically mercantile; money is its highest value. The enemy would *kū'ai hewa* "wrongfully sell out" (st. 3, l. 3) the natives' *pono sivila* "civil rights" (st. 3, l. 4).[141]

Hawaiian culture, on the other hand, is characterized by the fact that it does not *minamina* "value, cherish, care for" the *pu'ukālā* "hill of dollars" offered by the new government (st. 4, ll. 1f.). Hawaiians support the queen (st. 5, l. 1) and, by implication, their civil rights (st. 3, l. 4). But the poet sees an even more basic dimension in Hawaiian culture: the Hawaiian's relationship to the land, the natural *pu'u* "hill" rather than the hill of dollars. Hawaiians *kūpa'a* "stand firm" in support of the land (st. 1, l. 2). They want to obtain the pono of the land (st. 5, l. 2), an evocation of the saying of Kamehameha III. These actions are the result of the fact that Hawaiians are *ka po'e i aloha i ka 'āina* "the people who love the land" (st. 5, l. 5). In fact, the song was referred to as *Ke Mele Aloha 'Āina* "The Song of the Love of the Land."[142]

Western and Hawaiian values are confronted in stanza 4:

'A'ole mākou a'e minamina
I ka pu'ukālā a ke aupuni.

Ua lawa mākou i ka pōhaku
I ka 'ai kamaha'o o ka 'āina.

We do not value
The hill of dollars of the government.
We are satisfied with the rock,
The wondrous food of the land.

The dense image in lines 3–4 has been variously interpreted.[143] In my opinion, it is based on the expression '*ai pōhaku* "eat rock," used for someone who has nothing else.[144] The Hawaiians have been dispossessed and are reduced to what, for the non-Hawaiian, appears to be worthless. But the poet transforms this pejorative expression into a positive description of Hawaiian culture. The rock is *lawa* "enough, sufficient." The needs are basic. The rock is indeed '*ai* "food." That food is *kamaha'o*, a religious term used by Lunalilo in his anthem for the name of the king.

The Hawaiian eats the rock and is formed by it into a pua of Hawai'i. He brings the land inside of himself and thus becomes one with it. At the same time, the land becomes his. A chief is '*ai moku* "eater or ruler of the island or land section." The land is the Hawaiian's in the Hawaiian sense of tenancy or usufruct, rather than the Western sense of private property. That is, the Hawaiian rejects monetary prosperity in favor of sovereignty as defined by his own traditions.

A further source for this image—and a further dimension of its meaning—can be found in a traditional description of the volcano goddess Pele: *ka wahine 'ai pōhaku* "the rock-eating woman." She eats the rock and rules the lava flows and the lands around them. Pele also *produces* rock, *extends* the land. The Hawaiian also should give back to the land from which he receives. He should care for, *mālama*, his land. The relationship of humans to the land is, therefore, not one of exploitation or arbitrary rule, but of mutual care, of alternating receiving and giving.

Ultimately, the lines contain an authentic poetic symbol—that is, one that cannot be exhausted by interpretation but yields ever more to meditation. This is, in fact, an ideal of Hawaiian poetry: to reproduce in words the density of experience.

The difference between Hawaiian and Western culture is not, therefore, merely one of politics, but of perception and response. The use of such a symbol in such a situation is itself another point of difference between Hawaiian and Western culture and perpetuates the practice of using Hawaiian poetry as a screen, impenetrable to non-Hawaiians, behind which authentic indigenous concepts and feelings can be expressed.[145]

6.
A Politics of Beauty

The differences between Hawaiian and Western culture have been felt since first contact and have been examined by such writers as Kepelino. In the crisis of the overthrow of the monarchy, Lili'uokalani broached the subject of "the genius of a tropical people."[146]

> But will it also be thought strange that education and knowledge of the world have enabled us to perceive that as a race we have some special mental and physical requirements not shared by the other races which have come among us? That certain habits and modes of living are better for our health and happiness than others? And that a separate nationality, and a particular form of government, as well as special laws, are, at least for the present, best for us?[147]

Besides hospitality[148] and sensitivity to and dependence on nature,[149] she mentions "the great fondness and aptness of our nation to poetry and song."[150]

Poetry should be considered, therefore, an important source for our understanding of Hawaiian history. The fact that poetry has been used frequently for important occasions and purposes suggests that it has a utility thus far overlooked by historians. Moreover, the strong poetic bent of important public figures might not have been without influence on their views and policies. Indeed, my study of religio-political chants and songs indicates that poetry was felt in that field, just as it was in others, to be the most congenial form for the expression of feelings and philosophy. Only by achieving some appreciation of that poetry, I would argue, will we be able to understand the concerns and coherence of certain Hawaiian policies and tendencies. For instance the high, noble poetry of the Kalākaua dynasty renders comprehensible the place its members occupy in much contemporary Hawaiian thinking—a place that cannot be explained if only the literature of their English language detractors is studied. Ultimately, poetry has proved the best medium of expression for a primary factor in the thinking of Hawaiians as they confronted the problems of the postcontact period: their strong sense of the appropriateness of their traditional culture to the beautiful land they loved.

APPENDIX 1

The Use of Akua for Living Chiefs

Statements in nineteenth-century Hawaiian accounts that living chiefs of the highest rank were traditionally called *akua* "god" have been followed in the secondary literature (e.g., Davenport 1969:3, with references; Goldman 1970:218ff.). The historicity and/or exact extension and significance of this practice need, however, to be examined on the evidence of Hawaiian literature.

The use of akua for living high chiefs is well attested for the short period from the death of Kamehameha I through the early missionary period. See, for example, Stewart 1970:190; *He Kanikau no Kaahumanu Opio* "A Lamentation for Young Kaahumanu," by Niau, in Fornander 1919–1920:451–57; *Kalani nui kua Liholiho i ke kapu he inoa*, by Liliha, in *Buke Mele* n.d.:25f.; 25, ll. 1–4.

This use of akua is, however, difficult to demonstrate from earlier literature. For instance, Kamehameha I is clearly not an akua in the welcoming chant of Ululani discussed above, page 3. On the contrary, in *Haui Ka Lani* (Fornander 1919–1920: 409, ll. 769–74) Kamehameha I is *kanaka* "human"; *waiakua* "godly blood" (ibid.: 387f., ll. 299f.) preserves the distinction between Kamehameha I and akua. It could be objected that Kamehameha I was of insufficiently high rank to be called akua; but Kamakau (1961:230) claims that in the case of a victorious chief, "ua hoomana aku kekahi poe iaia me he akua la" (some people worshipped him as a god).* If akua was used as freely as claimed, the fact that the term was not applied to Kamehameha I must remain strange.

An even graver objection to the conventional position is that the claimed use of akua does not occur in earlier chants. (I agree with Dickey [1928:149] that the string figure chant line 5, *He akua na 'lii o Kona*, should be translated "ghosts"; compare *He Molelo* 1891, July 7,

---

*My translation from the Hawaiian text in *Ka Nupepa Kuokoa*, 16 November 1867, p. 1.

col. 2; Kahiolo 1978:61.) Such a use would certainly be expected in the earlier laudatory name chants of high chiefs, but the sole example of which I am aware, the chant in honor of Kūaliʻi, needs to be investigated in detail.

I accept the historicity of Kūaliʻi (vs. Beckwith 1970:395–99), even though few traditions about him survive. See, e.g., Sterling and Summers 1978:2, 10, 15, 37f., 61f., 135f., 140, 142, 178, 190, 238, 304f. I also accept the general authenticity of the chant for Kūaliʻi because it was collected from several sources (Fornander 1969:279 and n.1). However, the most explicit claim for the above use of akua is made in the prose accompanying the chant in the Fornander collection, *Moolelo o Kualii* "History of Kualii" in Fornander 1916–1917 (364–434; 365, 389 [along with Keawe of Hawaiʻi]; cf. 409, 411; Kamakau 1964:15). Lyons (1893:161) and Beckwith (1972:26) accept this claim.

The above-mentioned prose is by Kamakau (Fornander 1916–1917: 492, n. 2), who is also the source for other versions of the chant (see Fornander 1969:279 and n. 1; Lyons 1875:241) and was suspected of composing an original section added at the end of the chant (Lyons 1893:163; Fornander 1916–1917:394f., editor's note). Kamakau's prose story of Kūaliʻi seems to be an attempt to supply a tradition for that personage that could compare with other historical traditions preserved in the Fornander collection, such as the stories of the chiefs ʻUmi and Kawelo. For this purpose, traditional story motifs were used as well as attempted reconstructions of events from the chant itself (compare Fornander 1969:279f.). If the prose is indeed secondary, it can be used only with caution to interpret the chant.

Three passages pertain to the subject under discussion. Lines 149–59 in Fornander (1916–1917:375) seem to portray Kūaliʻi speaking in the first person about his trip to Tahiti (Kahiki in Fornander 1969:374). The people of Tahiti are not kānaka "normal human beings" but *haole* (a word later used for all non-Hawaiians) and akua. Lines 157–59:

Me ia la he akua,
Me aʻu la he kanaka;
He kanaka no.

He is like a god
I am like a human
A human indeed.

Here Kūaliʻi is explicitly kanaka rather than akua.

Lines 468–69 (Fornander 1916–1917:389) refer to Kūaliʻi:

Aole ia he kanaka.
O maua no na kanaka.

He is not a kanaka.
We two are indeed the kānaka.

The prose explains:

ua oleloia he akua o Kualii.

it was stated that Kūaliʻi was an akua.

The chant need not, however, be so interpreted. Previously, lines 427, 439, and 452, have repeated as a sort of refrain:

O Ku no ke alii.

Kū is indeed the chief.

The use of kanaka in lines 468–69 could be based then on the aliʻi/kanaka "chief/subject" distinction (as in Fornander 1916–1917:145) rather than on the akua/kanaka distinction.

The passage that contains the surest use of akua for Kūaliʻi in the chant is lines 593–94 (Fornander 1916–1917:395):

He kanaka ia,
He akua Ku . . .

This is a kanaka,
Kū is an akua . . .

The kanaka referred to seems to be Keawe, the chief of Hawaiʻi (l. 583). Kūaliʻi is exalted above him. The basis for calling Kūaliʻi an akua seems to be given in the next two lines (595f.):

He ulele Ku mai ka lani,
He haole Ku mai Tahiti . . .

Kū is a messenger from the sky,
Kū is a haole from Tahiti . . .

Haoles from Tahiti are akua, as seen above, lines 149–59. Confusingly, lines 597–99 read:

He mau kanaka ia eha.
Ewalu hoi nei kanaka,
O Ku, O Lono, O Kane, O Kanaloa . . .

These four are kānaka.
Eight are these kānaka,
Kū, Lono, Kāne, Kanaloa . . .

Akua and kanaka seem to be used idiosyncratically in this passage.
The chant of Kūaliʻi does not, therefore, provide sure evidence for the early use of akua for living chiefs. If a wider survey of Hawaiian literature fails to provide clear evidence of the usage in question, some modification of the conventional view is necessary. For instance, the question should be raised whether the nineteenth-century accounts are projecting a late usage onto an earlier period, or whether a genuine but restricted early usage was extended in later times.

Two passages from Kamakau (1961:208, 220) suggest that the usage under discussion may have been a novelty introduced by Kamehameha I himself:

O na keiki alii a imi haku wahi a Kamehameha, ua kapa aku no oia ia lakou he mau akua nona . . .

The children who were chiefly and sought leadership, by the statement of Kamehameha—he indeed called them some gods for him . . .

. . . . .

[Kamehameha would not call Liholiho his *keiki* "child," nor allow him to be so called by others.]

Eia hoi na hua e olelo aku ai imua ona, "ko Kahu, ko alii, ko moopuna, ko milimili, ko akua"

These indeed are the words that he would speak before him, "my [literally, your] guardian, my chief, my grandchild/descendant, my fondled one, my god."*

In both texts, especially the latter, Kamehameha's usage is presented not as normal or ordinary, but as an oddity worthy of note. This usage may prove to be a part of Kamehameha's restructuring of Hawaiian religion.

---

*My translations from the Hawaiian texts in *Ka Nupepa Kuokoa*, 7 September 1867, p. 1; and 21 September 1867, p. 1.

The Use of Akua for Living Chiefs

In two analogous passages (Kamakau 1961:312f., 318) Kamehameha's language is clearly presented as hyperbolic and figurative:

Ua hoolilo aku hoi o Kamehameha ia Kaahumanu i akua nona (wahi paha a ka olelo wale)

Indeed Kamehameha turned Kaʻahumanu into a god for himself (said perhaps only in talk).

. . . . .

Ua hilinai aku o Kamehameha ia Kaahumanu me he akua la nona, a me he lei niho palaoa la i ka a-i o Kamehameha

Kamehameha believed in Kaʻahumanu as if she were a god for him and as if she were a whale tooth necklace on the neck of Kamehameha.*

The relationship between the terms akua and kanaka is extremely varied and complex. The above discussion touches on only one aspect.

---

*My translations from the Hawaiian texts in *Ka Nupepa Kuokoa*, 19 September 1868, p. 1; and 26 September 1868, p. 1.

APPENDIX 2

Uses of Kapu and Kānāwai in Hawaiian Literature

Hawaiian law is an extensive and largely unexplored field. I will discuss only those points pertinent to the themes of this monograph, excluding, for instance, kānāwai "law" attached to things (e.g., Fornander 1916–1917:545); those that can best be described as customs, rules, and regulations with godly sanctions (Fornander 1919–1920:71, 115, 119, 137; Summers 1971: 199); and treaties (Kahiolo 1978:73, a valuable description of negotiating conditions for peace; cf. "He Molelo," 15 July 1891). I will give only a few examples for each point.

Legal terminology is not fully fixed. For instance, the uses of kapu "tabu" and kānāwai cannot be systematically distinguished. The kuaʻā "burning back" can be called both a kapu, as in the poem by Liliha cited in Appendix 1, and a kānāwai (Emerson 1915:231, l. 59). The phrase kānāwai kapu is found in Fornander (1919–1920:151; cf.41).

Laws, I would agree, were generally accompanied by a body of traditional information: the name of the law, its fixed formulation, the story of its origin, and the identification of its founder. The full complement can be found, for instance, in the extensive literature on Kamehameha I's *Māmala Hoa Kānāwai* "Law of the Splintered Paddle" (e.g., Fornander 1918–1919:469, 471; Kamakau 1961:125f., 181; Kamakau 1964:15; H. P. Judd 1930:40, no. 469). Kamakau (1961:62) possibly contains another example, although the phrase "lama kukui o Iwikauikaua" could be the name of the torches or of the event, rather than of the kapu privilege. Cf. Pukui 1983: no. 1904. Number 2556 may contain an example.

Some accounts provide only parts of this body of traditional information. Fornander (1916–1917:423) gives the name of a law's founder, the story of its foundation, and a fixed formulation, but no name for the law (cf. Kamakau 1961:231). For foundation stories with founder's name but no fixed formulations or names of the laws, see Summers (1971:200) and Sterling and Summers (1978:43, 54ff.). The name and story of a law are given without formulation or founder (folk origin?) in

Sterling and Summers (1978:23f.). Fornander (1916–1917:457) gives a fixed formulation and the person using the law (who might be the founder), but no foundation story. On formulations, compare Kahiolo 1978:73. On names of laws, see Fornander 1919–1920:423, 485; Pratt 1920:10f., 13, 17; Kamakau 1964: 11, 14, 22; Sterling and Summers 1978:243.

Laws could be standing (Kamakau 1961:182f.; Kamakau 1964:22), or be invoked on particular occasions—for instance, in order to spare prisoners (Fornander 1918–1919:693; Kamakau 1961:157; Kamakau 1964:11, 16f.; Sterling and Summers 1978:318)—or both, as the *Māmala Hoa Kānāwai*. Rules for the application of a law could be provided by tradition (Kamakau 1964:14).

In contrast to secondary literature, most Hawaiian language sources express positive views of laws (Kamakau 1961:369f.). They are a protection and a refuge (Kamakau 1964:11, 17). The kapu creates a *malu*, a shelter or protection (see above, p. 18; Green and Pukui 1936:58, *ko Kakuhihewa maluhia* "the 'king's peace' of Kakuhihewa"; and the references above to laws invoked to spare prisoners). The people are grateful to the chief for the law (Kamakau 1961:182f.).

Laws are, therefore, well known and appreciated. Their names give them a character and permanence in Hawaiian thinking, and their formulations are memorized the same way proverbs are. When a law is identified with a chief or god, it increases his or her prestige and can be mentioned as a reason for praise in laudatory chants (Kamakau 1961: 369; Fornander 1919–1920:423, 485; Emerson 1915:231; cf. McKinzie 1983:26–29, 91–94). A chief will cling to a kapu even in dire straits (Kamakau 1961:10; Sterling and Summers 1978:243) and can try to accumulate prestigious kapu and kānāwai (Kamakau 1961:223f.; Pratt 1920:10–13; McKinzie 1983:94). They can be given as recompense ([Buda] 1904:43).

Certain laws can be shared, such as the Burning Back tabu, claimed without controversy by several personages. Other laws can be the object of ownership disputes. Kamakau attributes the formulation of the *Māmala Hoa Kānāwai* to Kūali'i (Kamakau 1964:14; cf. Fornander 1918–1919:470, n. 16).

The *Kai 'Okia Kānāwai* "Law of the Cut Sea" is identified as an ancient swearing formula unconnected with a chief or god (Kamakau 1964:13f.). There was in fact a proverbial use of the phrase and its variants; see, for example, H. P. Judd 1930:38, no. 435; Fornander 1919–1920:455, l. 103; *Mele Aimoku* 1886:137, l. 5 from top; Poepoe 1891: 18, st. 4, l. 2 of Kalākaua's poem *Kalakaua Ia Kapiolani*; Pukui and Elbert 1971: see *moku* (1), on the phrase *kai moku* "cut sea."

The ownership of the law is, however, elsewhere attributed to the chief Lonoikamakahiki (Fornander 1916–1917:291). The law is also attributed to the god Kāne (Kamakau 1964:13f.; Fornander 1918–1919:296, l. 158, *A Lamentation for Kahahana*). A Pele chant claims the law for that goddess (Emerson 1915:228–31, l. 58; see also ibid.:40). Cf. Pukui 1983: no. 1410; Westervelt 1963:79. This chant has been used as a basis for arguing that the *Kai 'Okia Kānāwai* was originally Pele's, not Kāne's (Pukui in Kamakau 1964:22, n. 8; Barrère 1969:23f.). However, in the chant, the Pele worshipper is disputing the kapu privileges of other gods—especially Kāne and Kanaloa, who are driven away—and claiming kānāwai for his own god, Pele (ll. 37–47, 55–60). Appropriating for Pele a kānāwai that belonged originally to Kāne would, therefore, fit the tendency of the chant (Charlot 1983:23ff.). In all likelihood the *Kai 'Okia Kānāwai* is so ancient that it has become, on the one hand, proverbial and, on the other, subject to rival claims.

A further sign of the law's antiquity is the variety of interpretations offered of it. Kamakau (1964:13) gives the customary folk use as the sworn separation of two persons until death (cf. "He Molelo," 15 July 1891). The Lonoikamakahiki text, cited above, uses the law to separate people, such as war prisoners, from destruction (also Pukui and Elbert 1971: see *kai'okia*). Commenting on the text from *A Lamentation for Kahahana* (cited above and translated "Made sacred in the sea cut off by Kane"), Lorrin Andrews writes, "he is sacred to the sea, devoted first; okia a Kane, 'okia' for 'oki ia e,' cut off by Kane" (Fornander 1918–1919:303, n. 125). Pukui (1983: no. 1410) offers a similar interpretation, but applies the kānāwai to Pele, not Kāne. H. P. Judd (1930:38, no. 435) gives the interpretation, "The law is disregarded at sea." Kamakau (1964:13) also gives an interpretation based on the Biblical account of the flood.

Certain kapu and kānāwai, such as the Burning Back law, seem dependent on family connections and/or genealogical rank. Others can depend on historical circumstances, such as being born at a particularly sacred place (Sterling and Summers 1978:139f.). Other kapu and kānāwai are thought of as entities with effective power that is, to some degree, independent of gods or chiefs. For instance, Kamehameha I is pictured invoking a series of kānāwai before finally using one that is sufficiently powerful to produce the result he desires (Fornander 1918–1919:693; cf. Kamakau 1964:17). That is, the power of a kānāwai is to some degree distinguishable from that of the individual chief to whom it belongs. Kamehameha does not simply spare the prisoners on his own authority. Yet because of the traditional connection of a law to a chief, speculations were made that Kamehameha must possess a peculiar quality that enabled him to proclaim so powerful a law.

Apparently no theory was developed that accounted for both the personal and impersonal aspects of Hawaiian laws. A similar unresolved duality can be found in the related field of oaths. At times, an oath receives its sanction from a god (Kamakau 1964:13; Pukui and Elbert 1971: see *pau* (1), on the oath *Pau Pele, pau manō*). At other times, the oath itself appears to enforce observance (Fornander 1918–1919:581).

The connection of a famous, prestigious law to a chief helped ensure that he would enforce it. Godly rewards and punishments of the chief could also be persuasive (Kamakau 1964:15).

On the influence of precontact law on postcontact law, see, for example, Titcomb 1972:11–17. "He Molelo," 25 September 1891, seems to project a missionary regulation into the precontact past as a kānāwai.

APPENDIX 3

The Hawaiian National Anthems and Related Texts

I give in full those Hawaiian texts that are not generally available. I have retained the spelling and punctuation of the originals and have reproduced these wherever possible in my literal translations (all translations are mine except for the original English translation of E. O. Hall's *Restoration Anthem*). Stanza numbering has been regularized. Textual notes have been kept to a minimum. Arguments for my translations and interpretations are given in the main body of this monograph. Johnson 1975 was helpful in locating certain references from *Ka Nupepa Kuokoa*.

E. O. Hall: *Restoration Anthem*
Bille 1851:36f.

(Tune, 'God Save the King.') By Edwin O. Hall.

1	1
E ko makou alii!	Hail! to our rightful king!
Mahalo 'ka moi,	We joyful honors bring
I keia la!	This day to thee!
E mau kou ola nei!	Long live your majesty!
E mau kou aupuni!	Long reign this dynasty!
No na hanauna hoi,	And for posterity
I oni paa.	The sceptre be!

2	2
Nani! ka inoa maikai!	Hail! to the worthy name!
Me kona aina nae!	Worthy his Country's Fame
Toma ke koa!	Thomas, the brave!
Mahalo 'kou maikai,	Long shall thy virtues be
Kou wikiwiki mai!	Shrined in our memory,
Maluna o ke kai,	Who came to set us free,
E kuu 'na paa.	Quick o'er the wave!

3
Hiilani i ke Lii!
Iehova ka Moi,
  E hapai no;
Nui ke kupinai!
Nui ke mele nae!
I mau ka pomaikai
  Ia oe no.

3
Praise to our Heavenly King!
To Thee our thanks we bring,
  Worthy of all;
Loud we thine honors raise!
Loud is our song of praise!
Smile on our future days,
  Sovereign of all!

Honolulu, Oahu, Iulai 31, 1843. Honolulu, Oʻahu, July 31, 1843.

The following is a more literal translation:

1
Oh our chief!
Thanks to the king,
  On this day!
May your life here endure!
May your government endure!
For the generations also,
  May it act from a firm foundation.

2
Beautiful! the good name!
With his country also!
  Thomas, the warrior!
Thanks for your goodness,
Your speed in coming here!
Over the sea,
  To let go the bound.

3
Praise to the Chief!
Jehovah the King,
  Raise up [our voices];
Great is the noise!
Great also the singing!
So prosperity may endure
  Through you indeed.

Hall's anthem commemorated the return of Hawaiian sovereignty by Great Britain through Admiral Thomas (L. F. Judd 1928:102f.; Richards 1970:188f., 191, 194, 196). In 1845, Hall's work was referred to as the national anthem (Richards 1970:230). Bille (1851:36) calls it a "patriotisk Hymne."

Announcement of the Contest for a National Anthem
The following announcement appeared on 16 December 1861 in *Ka Nupepa Kuokoa*, p. 2. I have left typographical errors uncorrected.

He Mele Hou no ke 'Lii o kakou!
$10.00 Makana!
Eia ka mea i makemakeia, he mea e lealea ai na kanaka Hawaii, ka poe aloha aku i ka Moi. Ua makemakeia ke mele hou no keia lahuikanaka e hapai i ke Alii a i ke 'Lii Wahine a me ka Haku o Hawaii. He mele no ko Beretania, pela no ko Farani, pela hoi ko Amerika e hookaulana ai; e pono hoi i mele e hiilani ai ko Hawaii i ko lakou Moi.

E haawi no wau i dala no kekahi mele olelo Hawaii ua oi aku ka maikai o ka haku ana, e like nae me ke mele Beretane, "Na ke Akua e hoola i ke Alii," (God save the King.) A eia na rula o ka haku ana.

1. O ka mea nana i haku he hanauna Hawaii, (kanaka maoli.)

2. E hanaia mamua o ka la 31 o Ianuari, 1862, no ka mea, ma ia hope aku, aole e aeia ke mele ke laweia mai, e imi i ka makana. A, no ka mea, e pai ana ke mele no ka la hanau o ka Moi, Feb. 9, 1862.

3. E waeia i ekolu poe noiau e nana a e hooholo i ke mele maikai noloko mai o ka lehulehu, a e pai ana na inoa oia poe maloko o ke *Kuokoa* e puka mai ana.

4. E haawiia NA DALA HE UMI i ka mea mele oi loa o ka maikai, ke hooholoia nae e na poe Lunanana i kohohoia he kupono ka uku aku i ka makana.

5. I eha wale no pauku o ke mele, a e like loa ke pili ana i ka leo, *God save the King*.

6. E pili loa ke mele hou ma ke ano o ka olelo o ke mele i paiia malalo.

Eia kekahi mele Beretane, i ike ia'i ka ano o ka hana ana i na pauku ma ka olelo Hawaii.

Tune—*God Save the King*.

1
God bless our chosen King,
Long live this nation's King,
  God bless the King!
Keep him from harm secure,
Wise, faithful, honored, pure,
Long may his throne endure,
  God Save the King!

2
Now in our hymn of praise,
A gentler name we raise,
  God bless the Queen!

Oh! may that noble love,
Her people's sorrows prove,
Reflected from above,
   But bless the Queen!

3
And may their royal heir
Thy choicest blessings share,
   God bless the Prince!
Do Thou his path defend!
Thy peace his steps attend!
Thy word his constant friend,
   God Bless the Prince!

4
Crowned by their people's love,
Guarded by Heaven above,
   Long may they reign!
And when their race is run,
A nobler crown have won,
The gift of Thee alone,
   Great King of Kings!

A eia malalo nei ke ano o ke mele i paiia maluna ua hoololiia:

Pauku 1.—E hoomaikai, e ke Akua, i ko makou Alii, a e loihi kona ola ana. Ke Akua e hoomaikai i ko makou Moi. E nana iaia maikahi poino, noho malie, naauao, hoopono, mahalo, a halaole. E loihi kona noho Alii ana. Ke Akua e hoola i ka Moi.

Pauku 2.—Ano i ka kakou mele, he inoa hou ka kakou e oli nei, ke Akua e hoola i ka Moi Wahine. E hoike ae ia i kona aloha kiekie no ke kaumaha o kona poe kanaka, ke olinolino mai luna o ka lani. Ke Akua e hoola i ka Moi Wahine.

Pauku 3.—E loaa hoi i ke keiki alii ka hoomaikaiia e ke Akua, e hoomaikai i ka Haku o Hawaii, na ke Akua e kiai i kona alanui, a e malama i kona mau keehi ana, a e lilo hoi ka oiaio hemolele o ke Akua, i aikane mau loa nana. Ke Akua e hoomaikai i ka Haku o Hawaii.

Pauku 4.—Hoaliiia e ko na kanaka aloha, a kiaiia hoi e ka lani i luna. E loihi ko lakou noho alii ana; a i ko lakou make ana. E loaa ia lakou ke Kalaunu ma ka lani, ka makana au wale no, ke Alii nui o na 'Lii.

Auhea oukou e ka poe Hawaii nei i akamai i ke kakau mele, aia mai ka hana na oukou, he hana nana e hoike i kou inoa, a e hoomanaoia'i e kou lahuikanaka.

O na mea a pau e kakau ana i keia mele makana, e pono e kena mai ia'u i ko lakou inoa ma kekahi palapala e ae i wepaia a paa, me ke mele pu maloko. Aole e weheia ka inoa, aia a pau ka hai ana o na Luna nana i ka lakou olelo hooholo.

E paiia ka inoa o ua poe Luna la ma ke *Kuokoa* i keia hoopuka ana 'e.

H. M. Wini.
Luna Pai o ka Nupepa Kuokoa.

A New Song for our Chief!
$10.00 Prize

This is what is wanted, something to please Hawaiians, the people who love the King. The new song is wanted for this race to praise the Chief and the Chiefess and the Prince of Hawai'i. The British have a song, so have the French, and so also, the Americans, to make their countries famous; it is right also that there be a song with which the Hawaiians can praise their King.

I will give dollars for the best composed Hawaiian-language song which resembles the British song "It is God's to give life to the Chief," (God save the King.) Here are the rules of composition:

1. The composer must be of Hawaiian birth (native Hawaiian).

2. It must be done before January 31, 1862, because, after that, the songs received will not be accepted as contestants for the prize. The reason for this is that the song will be published for the King's birthday, Feb. 9, 1862.

3. Three skilled people will be chosen to examine and decide on the right song from among the many, and the names of these people will be published in a future number of the *Kuokoa*.

4. 10 DOLLARS will be given to the composer of the best song, if the selected judges, in fact, decide that the prize should be awarded.

5. There should be only four stanzas to the song, and it should adhere closely to the tune, *God save the King*.

6. The new song should adhere closely to the sense of the text of the song printed below.

Here is a British song, in which can be seen the sense of the work to be done in the Hawaiian-language stanzas.

[God Save the King.]

Here below is the sense of the song printed above; it has been translated:

[Hawaiian-language paraphrase.]

Attention, you Hawaiians who are clever at composing songs, here is a task for you, a work which will make your name known and remembered by your race.

All you who write a prize song should send me their names on another paper, tightly sealed, together with the song inside. The name will not

be opened until the examining judges have finished announcing their decision.
The judges' names will be published in a future issue of the *Kuokoa*.

H. M. Whitney
Editor, *Ka Nupepa Kuokoa*.

Announcement of the Names of the Contest Judges
Ka Nupepa Kuokoa, 25 January 1862, p. 2

KE MELE UKU.—E like me ka makou hoolaha ana ma ka Helu 5, ua loaa mai ia makou na mele he nui wale. Hookahi wale no nae mele e loaaʻi ka uku i oleloia, oia ke mele maikai loa o lakou. Ekolu mea i kohoia i mau Luna nana e hooholo i ke mele kupono ke uku ia, a me ka pono ole paha, o ka uku ana no kekahi o ia mau mele a pau. O na mea nona na inoa malalo nei ka poe luna i kohoia.

James I. Dowsett, (Kimo Pelekane.)
G. P. Judd, (Kauka.)
E. O. Hall, (Mi Holo.)

E pono i na mea mele ke hooili mai, mamua aku o ka la mua o Febeari, i paiiaʻi ma ka Helu 11, i ka la mamua iho o ka la hanau o ka moi.

THE PRIZE SONG.—Conforming to our announcement in Number 5, we have received very many songs. However, only one song will receive the prize mentioned, that is, the best song of those received. Three people have been chosen as examining Judges to decide on the song worthy of being awarded the prize, or [to decide] that it is not right to award the prize to any of all these songs. The people whose names are given below are the selected judges.
[The names with Hawaiian forms or nicknames.]
Composers should submit their works before February 1 to be published in Number 11, on the day before the birthday of the king.

William Charles Lunalilo: *E Ola ka Mōʻī i ke Akua*
Ka Nupepa Kuokoa, 8 February 1862, p. 1. Also in Smith 1955a:18, with intercalated English translation.

E ola ka Moi i ke Akua.
Hakuia e WM. C. LUNALILO.

1
Ke Akua mana mau,
Hoomaikai, pomaikai
I ka Moi!

1
God of enduring power,
Bless, make prosper
The King!

Kou lima mana mau,
Malama, kiai mai,
  Ko makou nei Moi
    E ola e!

2
Ka inoa Kamahao,
Lei nani o makou,
    E ola e!
Ko Eheu uhi mai,
Pale na ino e,
Ka makou pule nou
    E ola e!

3
Haliu, maliu mai,
Nana mai luna mai
  Kau Pokii nei;
E mau kou ola nei,
Ke Akua kou kiai
Ka Pua nani e
  Hawaii nei!

4
Imua Ou makou,
Ke 'Lii o na 'Lii,
  E aloha mai;
E mau ka Ea nei
O keia Aupuni.
E ola mau lakou,
  Ia oe no.

Ianuari 4, 1862.

Your hand of enduring power,
Care for, guard
  Our King here
    May he live!

2
The Wondrous name,
Beautiful *lei* of ours,
    May he/she live!
May your Wings cover [us],
Ward off the evils,
Our prayer for you
    May he/she live!

3
Turn, turn this way,
Look here from above
  Your Younger Brother here;
May your life endure,
God be your guard
The beautiful Flower
  [Of] Hawai'i here!

4
We come before You,
The Chief of Chiefs,
  Give us your love;
May the Life-Breath endure here
Of this Government.
May they live,
  Through you indeed.

January 4, 1862.

William Charles Lunalilo: *E Ola ka Mō'ī i ke Akua*, **second version**
Ka Nupepa Kuokoa, 11 January 1873, p. 2; also in Johnson 1976:344. This version was used on Lunalilo's accession to the throne. Unless specifically noted, all references are to the first version.

E OLA KA MOI I KE AKUA!
God Save the King.
Leo "America"

1
Ke Akua mana mau
Hoomaikai, pomaikai
  I ka Moi!

1
God of enduring power
Bless, make prosper
  The King!

Kou lima mana e,	Your powerful hand,
Malama, kiai mai	Care for, guard
I ko makou Moi,	Our King,
E ola e!	May he live!

2

Ka inoa kamahao	The wondrous name
E Lunalilo e,	Oh Lunalilo,
E ola mau!	Live forever!
Lei nani o makou,	Beautiful *lei* of ours,
Maliu aloha mai;	Turn lovingly this way;
I kou Lahui nei	To your People/Race here
E ola e!	May he/it live!

3

Na ke 'Lii o na 'Lii,	It is the Chief of Chief's
E poni i Moi;	To anoint a King;
No ka Lahui	For the People/Race
E mau ke ea nei	May this life-breath endure
O ke Aupuni ou	Of your Government
Ka makou pule nou	This is our prayer for you
E ola e!	May he/it live!

Jno. I. Nā'ili'ili: *Na ke Akua e Ho'ōla i ka Mō'ī!*
Ka Nupepa Kuokoa, 1 March 1862, p. 3. In an accompanying letter, the author states that he did not submit his song in time for the contest because he had written it out of affection for the king and was uninterested in the prize.

Na ke Akua e hoola i ka Moi!	*It is God's to give life to the King!*
Leo "God Save the King"	Tune "God Save the King"

1

Ke Akua nani e,	Oh beautiful God,
Kokua o launa,	Help greatly,
I ke Alii!	The chief!
Nau no e kiai mai,	Yours it is indeed to guard,
Nau no e hoopomaikai,	Yours it is indeed to bless,
I ko makou Alii,	Our chief,
I ola mau!	So that he may live forever!

2

Ka Moi Wahine,	The Queen,
Kau e hoopomaikai,	Come to bless,
I ola ai!	So that she live!
E hoonui ae hoi,	Increase also,

I kana mau hua,
I lehulehu ai,
   A ola mau!

3
Keia Kamaiki nei,
Kau e malama mai,
   I ola mau!
Hoolilo ae ia ia,
I mea kupaa mau,

Ma ka Noho Moi,
   A mau loa!

4
E hookupaa mai,
I keia Aupuni,
   I onipaa!

E mau ae ke ola,
E mau ka maluhia,
E ola lakou nei,
   Ke Akua mau!

Jno. I. Nailiili
Honolulu, Dek. 17, 1861

Her fruits,
So they may be many,
   And live forever!

3
This Little Boy here,
Come to care for him,
   So that he may live forever!
Turn him,
Into a person who stands enduringly firm,
On the Throne,
   Forever!

4
Make stand firm,
This Government,
   So that it may act from a firm foundation!
May life endure,
May peace endure,
May these people live,
   [Through the] Eternal God!

Jno. I. Nāʻiliʻili
Honolulu, Dec. 17, 1861

Peter K. Kaleikini: no title
Ka Nupepa Kuokoa, 29 March 1862, p. 1

Leo Mele "God Save the King." *Song Tune "God Save the King."*

1
Ke Akua e hoomaikai
I ko makou Alii!
   E ola mau.
E mau kou ola nei,
E mau kou Aupuni.
Mai ke Akua mai
   E ola ke ʻLii.

2
Ke mele nei makou
I ka Moi Wahine!
   Ke Akua e hoola.
E hai i kou aloha

1
God bless
Our Chief!
   May he live forever.
May your life here endure,
May your government endure.
Through God
   May the Chief live.

2
We sing
To the Queen!
   God give her life.
Express your love

I kou poe kanaka.
Ke Akua e hoola
   Ke 'Lii Wahine.

3
Ke Akua e hoomaikai
I ka hooilina Alii,
   Ka Haku Hawaii!
Na ke Akua e kiai
I kou mau kapuai.
Ke Akua e hoomaikai
   Ke 'Lii Opio.

4
Na na kanaka hoi
I koho ia oukou,
   E noho Alii.
Ka Lani e kiai
Ko oukou Aupuni.
Ao [No] na hanauna a pau
   I oni paa.

To your native people.
God give life
   To the Queen.

3
God bless
The Chiefly successor,
   The Prince of Hawai'i!
It is God's to guard
Your steps.
God bless
   The Young Chief.

4
By the people indeed
You were chosen,
   To reign as Chiefs.
May the Lord guard
Your Government.
For all generations
   May it act from a firm foundation.

Ao in stanza 4, line 6 yields no clear sense. I emend the text to *No*, which could have easily been misread in typesetting. Kaleikini's wording is heavily dependent on the *Kuokoa* prose translation of *God Save the King* and on E. O. Hall's *Restoration Anthem*. Kaleikini's stanza 1, lines 4–5, correspond literally to Hall's lines at the same locus. Kaleikini has then moved Hall's next two lines to the end of his own anthem (st. 4, ll. 6ff.), changing only Hall's *ho'i* to *a pau*.

J. P. Kāneali'i: no title
Ka Nupepa Kuokoa, 29 March 1861, p. 1.

Tune—"God Save the King."

1
E ke Akua e,
Kapuuhonua mau
   E malu ai.
Malama i ka Moi
O keia lahui.
E ola ka Moi
   Hawaii nei.

1
Oh God,
Enduring sanctuary
   In which to be at peace.
Take care of the King
Of this people.
May the King live
   [Of] Hawai'i here.

2	2
Hoolea kakou nei,	We rejoice,
I ke Akua mau	Through the eternal God
E ola ai.	To live.
I ola pomaikai,	May live prosperously,
Ka Moi Wahine,	The Queen,
A lanakila mau	And be constantly victorious
I keia ao.	In this world.

3
Akua mana mau,   God of enduring power,
Hoomaikai i ka Haku   Bless the Prince
  Hawaii nei.   [Of] Hawai'i here.
Ke Kamakahi e,   The Only Son,
Aloha nui mai.   Give us your great love.
E ola ka Haku   May the Prince live/So that the Prince may live
  Hawaii nei.   [Of]Hawai'i here.

4
E mau no hoi lakou,   May they indeed endure,
Na hanau[n]a Moi   The Royal family
  Hawaii nei.   [Of] Hawai'i here.
Kau ke Karaunu hou,   May a new Crown be placed [on them],
Na Iesu i hoomaikai,   Blessed by Jesus,
E ola na Moi   May the Royalties live
  Hawaii nei.   [Of] Hawai'i here.

Hawai'i: *He Mele no nā Li'i*
Ka Nupepa Kuokoa, 24 May 1862, p. 1

Leo—"God save the King."   Tune—"God save the King."

1
E hoomaikaiia mai   May be blessed
Ko kakou 'lii maikai,   Our good chief,
  Ka Moi nei;   The King here;
E ola ka Moi,   May the King live,
E paa kou noho 'lii,   May your throne be secure,
Hee ae na enemi,   May the enemies retreat,
  A malu e.   And there be peace.

2	2
Kou hoa maikai e	Your good companion
Ke 'Lii Wahine nei,	The Chiefess here,
E ola pu;	May she live together [with you];
E hooloihiia'e	May be lengthened
Ko laua pomaikai,	The prosperity of both,
Na Moi akamai,	The intelligent Royalties,
Koonei Hoku.	Stars of this place.
3	3
Hoomaikai pu ia'e	May be blessed together [with them]
Ka Haku maka mae,	The precious Prince,
Ka Moi hou;	The new King;
E lilo o ia nei	May he become
I Moi pololei,	A King correct,
A hanohano e,	And glorious,
I oli kakou.	So we may be happy.
4	4
E hoohauoli mai	May the good Chief of above
Ko luna Alii maikai,	Make happy
I na Moi;	The Royalties;
E mau ke Aupuni e	May the Government endure
O ko Hawaii nei,	Of [the chiefs] of Hawai'i here,
Hookani nui ae,	Raise high our voices,
E ola na 'Lii.	May the chiefs live.
Hawaii.	Hawai'i.

Lili'uokalani: *He Mele Lāhui Hawai'i*
"A Song of the Hawaiian People/Race"
Elbert and Mahoe 1970:47f.

See Lili'uokalani 1964:31f. I disagree with the Elbert and Mahoe text of chorus, line 3, which is given as:

A mākou mana nui

Our great power.

Lili'uokalani (1897: unnumbered) gives this clearly as *ma kou* "in your [God's]." Her translation, on page 2, does not include the chorus. Parallel to the reading *ma kou* are: chorus, l. 2; st. 2, l. 7; st. 3, ll. 1, 8. Smith (1955a:19) reads *ma kou* and translates "And by Thy great power." The reading is important for the interpretation of the anthem.

Anonymous: *He Himeni i haku 'ia no ka Mō'ī D. Kalākaua*
"A Hymn composed for the King D. Kalākaua"
Ka Nupepa Kuokoa, 20 June 1874, p. 4

He Himeni i haku ia no ka
Moi D. Kalakaua.
America 6–4.

<table>
<tr><td>

1
E Kalakaua e,
Kokua ia makou,
  I pomaikai,
Ko makou Moi hou,
Mai Hawaii a Kauai,
A Kuikahi pu,
  Makou a pau.

2
Ua lanakila no,
Ka inoa maikai ou,
  Maluna ae,
O ke aupuni nei,
Ua pau na ino e,
Ua kau ka lei alii,
  Maluna ou.

3
Ke pule nei makou,
I ke Akua mau,
  E ola e,
E mau kou ola nei,
Me na'lii no a pau,
Makaainana pu,
  Mai o a o.

</td><td>

1
Oh Kalākaua,
Help us,
  To be blessed,
Our new King,
From Hawai'i to Kaua'i,
And unite together,
  All of us.

2
Conquered indeed,
Has your good name,
  Over,
This government,
The evils are done with,
The chiefly *lei* has been placed,
  On you.

3
We pray,
The eternal god,
  May he live,
May your life here endure,
With all the chiefs,
Together with the people of the land,
From this place to that.

</td></tr>
</table>

He Himeni is quoted in an article "Hoike o ke kula Sabati o Siloama Kalawao Molokai" (Public Examination of the Sabbath school of Siloama Church, Kalawao, Moloka'i), in which the program of *ha'awina*, assigned lessons to be demonstrated, is given. *He Himeni* was probably not meant as a title, but I will so use it for convenience.

Smith (1955b:14) called attention to this work, which he attributed to Kalākaua himself; he based his conclusion on an unfortunate mistranslation of "haku ia *no* ka Moi," which he rendered "written *by* the King" (italics mine). The correct translation of "for" instead of "by" would indicate that the song had not been composed by Kalākaua. Moreover, throughout the article, the phrases *haku 'ia, himeni haku,* and so on, seem to indicate original compositions by the school members being examined. The three other songs quoted are so designated. Of the songs mentioned without such a designation, all but two are provided with references to one of the mission hymn books, *Lira Kamalii, Ka Lira Hawaii,* or *Ka hae hoonani.* I would conclude that *He Himeni* was not composed by Kalākaua but by someone at the school in his honor. It is, however, as I will show in the text of this monograph, based on previous anthems and the themes of the Kalākaua propaganda and campaign literature.

Smith has changed the punctuation. I disagree with the period he places after *aʻe* (st. 2, l. 3), which leaves the phrase *Maluna aʻe* with no secure syntactical place.

Kalākaua: *Hawaiʻi Ponoʻī* "Hawaiʻi's Own"
Elbert and Mahoe 1970:43f.

The story of the composition of this anthem has been told many times (e.g., Smith 1956b).

Notes

1. On tension, see Rémy 1859:10f., 40; Beaglehole 1967:543, 550, 560, 564. On the similarity between priests and chiefs, see Rémy 1862:162; Fornander 1916-1917:239. Priest and chief are coordinated in ceremony, as seen in Titcomb 1972:43f.; also Malo 1951:53, 189f.; Kamakau 1976:91; Fornander 1919-1920:11, 19, 37, 121. Other examples of this can be found.

"Priestly" functions can be performed by non-priests such as farmers (Handy and Handy 1972:387, 580ff.), heads of family (ibid.:297, 301, 317f.), and fishermen (Kamakau 1976:85). Priestly and chiefly offices can be, and in important cases were, united in one person. See Kamakahelei, *Mele Inoa no Kihapiilani* "Name Song for Kihapiilani," in Fornander 1919-1920:411-415, 413, line 69: *He kahuna 'o ka lani* "The chief is a priest." See also Kamakau 1961:117, 153, 187f.(?); Kirtley and Mookini 1977:51. The most famous case is Kamehameha I, who held the positions of high priest and high chief. For an example of his religious activity, see Kamakau 1961:140f., 185.

The historical relationships between chiefs and priests provide a background against which to understand the 1819 abolition of the *kapu* system by the government of Kamehameha II. Līloa bequeathed his chiefly power to the unloved Hākau and bequeathed his god, Kāʻilimoku, to the beloved ʻUmi. Later, after slowly gathering support, ʻUmi won through revolution the chiefly power. Kalaniʻōpuʻu bequeathed his station and most of his lands to the weak Kiwalaʻō and the god Kāʻilimoku to Kamehameha I, who again through revolution later assumed supreme power. At his death, Kamehameha I left the government to the weak Liholiho (Kamehameha II), who was dominated by the court chiefesses, and left the god, now named Kūkāʻilimoku, to his favorite nephew, the admired Kekuaokalani. Kamehameha I had carefully instructed the two in the history of such a partition (Kamakau 1961:209; see also pp. 9, 109, 118f.). Such precedents could not be ignored. The abolition of the kapu system by Kamehameha II's regents was, I would argue, an attempt to deprive Kekuaokalani of his power base and to precipitate, along with other actions, a conflict before he had time to gather support.

Most Westerners of the nineteenth century would not have separated religion, politics, and culture as clearly as contemporary Americans do (e.g., Armstrong 1977:53, 64, 101ff., 149f., 157, 180, 280). Compare the view of the converted Kaʻahumanu (Kamakau 1961:328f.). Differences between Protestants and Roman Catholics quickly became factors in chiefly rivalries (e.g., Richards 1970:30, 39).

2. See the theory of Kamakau in Beckwith 1970:295f. Also Handy and Handy 1972:309. For secondary treatments of this subject, see Davenport 1969:6-8; Goldman 1970:200-242; Elbert 1956-1957. My views are nearest to those of Elbert because he bases himself on Hawaiian language sources, including literature, and therefore avoids systematizing.

3. The most complete example from Hawaiian culture is the *Kumulipo* (Beckwith 1972; Malo 1951:55).

4. See *Birth Chant for Kau-i-ke-ao-uli* in Pukui and Korn 1973:12–28, 198–204. An example of the chief's actions being discussed in cosmic terms can be found in Pukui 1983: no. 1421.

5. Kamakau 1961:133f.; Pukui 1983: no. 756; Handy and Handy 1972:351. A proverbial case is that of the evil chief Hua. See also *Haui Ka Lani* by Keʻāulumoku in Fornander 1919–1920:368–410; 397, ll. 473–79; 398f., ll. 481–515 (Kamehameha's reign is compared to a great, peaceful feast for all the islands); 403, ll. 598, 610–17; 404f., ll. 637–57 (Kamehameha's reign enjoys a peace and prosperity similar to those established by the great chiefs of old); 408, ll. 738–50. See also Rémy 1862:142. *Birth Chant for Kau-i-ke-ao-uli* (see above n. 4) views the unusually painful labor as a symptom of civil and cosmic disorder (Charlot 1983:109–12). See also Elbert 1959:207:

> No ka mea, pela e ola ai ko olua haku. Ina ola ia, ola kakou, ina make ia, make kakou.

> Because in that way your chief will live. If he lives, we live. If he dies, we die.

The solidarity between chief and people is a major theme of "He Molelo Kaao no Kamapuaa" 1891 (e.g., July 29, 30); I have examined it in Charlot, forthcoming.

6. Fornander 1919–1920:387, l. 284.

7. Ibid.:404, ll. 635f. The translation in the published text is:

> Clearly plain is the welfare of the land,
> The chief has established his authority . . .

I kea may be a typographical error for *'ikea*, in which case the translation would be: "Clearly seen is the rightness of the land." Cf. 404, ll. 634ff. For a similar antithesis, see 372, ll. 58f.

On Keʻāulumoku, see Kamakau 1961:89f., 112–15, 122f., 126, 394(?); Kalākaua 1972:351–67. I have found the following poems attributed to him:

> *Ouiui a Waʻa-kia-loa ke kane*, Kamakau 1961:89f.
> *Alo-ha, alo-ha*, Kamakau 1961: 112–15.
> *Haui Ka Lani*, Fornander 1919–1920:368–410; *Na Mele Aimoku* 1886:42–76. English translation also in Dole 1875. Fornander 1969:156; Kamakau 1961:122f., 126, 350.
> *Ka Pule Kumu O Alalala-he, ke Akua*, Beckwith 1932:35, 182–86. Barrère 1969:21.
> *E Ninau Mai Ana Ka Oe, Na Mele Aimoku* 1886:279f.
> *'Auʻa 'Ia, Na Mele Aimoku* 1886:3–7(?); 304f. There are obvious textual problems. Shorter variants are used for hula today.

The attribution of the *Kumulipo* to him is erroneous (Beckwith 1972:25).

8. Fornander 1919–1920:409, l. 769; cf. ll. 770f. This sense of pono can be found also in Pratt 1920:63, l. 22: *Pono no i Kuamoo o Haloa* "Right indeed in the line of Hāloa."

9. Fornander 1919–1920:444–50; 444, ll. 11–14. For *kū[k]aʻi*, see ibid.:444, n. 13. The published text uses both the name-like *Kalani* and *ka lani*, emphasizing the reference to both sky and chief.

Because the existence of materials authored by Nāhiʻenaʻena has recently been denied (Sinclair 1976:78f.), I would like to call attention to the following documents, which I have found in the course of my research on other subjects. This is by no means intended as an exhaustive list.

a. A deposition by Nāhi'ena'ena in Hawaiian, with appended English translation, and other documents relating to a case of prostitution (Sinclair 1976:89). Hamilton Library, University of Hawaii, Microfilm 709, Reel 3, *A.B.C.F.M.*, *Letters and Papers*. *Hawaiian Islands Mission* (first page on microfilm: *Letters and Papers of the Board*, vol. 32, Sandwich Islands Mission, part 2. [Received between June 20, 1828, and Aug. 27, 1830]). This letter was noted by Morris, Young, Kahapea, and Yamanaka 1974:38.

b. A letter in English to Stewart, dated Lahaina, 31 May 1828, on the same microfilm. "No. 218" is printed at the top of the sheet. I have not checked the entire reel.

c. Seven chants by Nāhi'ena'ena are copied in *Buke Mele* n.d.:1f., 18ff., 48, 118f., 136.

Esther K. Mookini recently brought to my attention the newspaper article "He Manao Aloha" 1834. Other such articles can in all likelihood be found.

10. Fornander 1919-1920:460-69; 468, ll. 260-65. Compare the first line cited with Pukui 1983: no. 1412. The last two lines cited seem to be playing on the saying in Pukui 1983: no. 540. Cf. *Haui Ka Lani*, Fornander 1919-1920:386f., ll. 282-300. The chief's close association with his people and his lack of pretention are qualities admired in other chants, for example *Lunalilo* (Fornander 1919-1920:534). Lunalilo himself expressed the view that his election demonstrated the solidarity between himself and his people (Johnson 1976: 342, 344). Cf. Kamakau 1961:142f., 205; Beckwith 1932:141; Korn 1958:170. Mrs. Lou Cestere of Kahana Valley, O'ahu, told me that she had been impressed that Prince Kūhiō in his election campaigns had not restricted himself to his circle of noble friends, but had mingled freely and easily with the common people.

11. I will discuss this relationship several times in this monograph. See above note 9. See also Pukui 1983: nos. 1149, 1213. Kamakau (1961) regularly refers to this relationship, e.g., pp. 369-72. See also Lili'uokalani 1964:2f., 195 (the relationship between higher and lower chiefs), 212f., 231, 370; cf. 169. Johnson 1976:281; 344, st. 2, ll. 5ff. of the anthem. Cf. Beaglehole 1967:613. Charles de Varigny (1874:295f.) describes the relationship between Kamehameha V and his subjects as one of aloha and mutual respect, along with a preservation of distinctions; also, ibid.:306, 308.

The historian Homer A. Hayes communicated privately to me two maxims on "the ancient obligation of *ali'i*," given to him by his mother, the Hawaiian political leader and Republican legislator Flora Ka'ai Hayes: "The chief must aloha those who make it possible for him to be what he is"; and "Take good care of those who make possible what you are." This seems to be a version of Pukui 1983: no. 1150; cf. nos. 1172, 1185.

Songs of praise and affection were often composed by subjects on the occasion of their chief's visit (e.g., Pukui and Korn 1973:73-79, 210f.). Compare the saying in Pukui 1983: no. 2452. Chiefs who burden the people occasion rebellion. See *Na Alii Hooluhi o Kau* "The Despotic Chiefs of Kau," Green 1926:86-91; Pukui 1983: no. 2451. Compare the charge that the rebelliousness occasioned by Kalākaua's rule is a symptom of its incorrectness (Johnson 1976:417). A young commoner expressed neatly the traditional attitudes toward chiefs: "Good Queen make good people"; and "too much chief eat up people!" (Bird 1966:65). Cf. Pukui 1983: no. 2450.

12. *Haui Ka Lani*, in Fornander 1919-1920:373, l. 71.

13. Malo 1951:55, 75, 189f.; Kamakau 1961:9, 34f., 117, 133f., 167, 182, 221ff., 258, 261, 369; Rémy 1862:142. *Haui Ka Lani* repeatedly emphasizes Kamehameha I's piety, Fornander 1919-1920:378f., ll. 152-65; 401ff., ll. 547-605, 609; 404, ll. 620-25; 405, ll. 658-69 (Kamehameha's warrior activity is interpreted as religious); 407, ll. 702ff.

14. Rémy 1862:142. Cf. Kamakau 1961:226; Pukui 1983: no. 2451.

15. Pukui and Korn 1973:10, l. 10. See also ibid.:9ff., 197f. Cf. *Haui Ka Lani*, in Fornander 1919-1920:378, l. 155. The relationship is more often reversed, for example, Fornander 1919-1920:11: the chief says to the god, *e ola au ia oe* "may I live through you"; cf. ibid.:19.

16. The correspondence between Queen Emma and Peter Kaeo provides much information on these ideas. See, e.g., Korn 1976:168, 255f. (genealogy and family); 78, 208f., 232, 237, 242, 259 (proper chief and social and cosmic harmony).

17. See Appendix 1.

18. For instance, in Ekaula (1865:1) the members of Kamehameha V's genealogy are called upon as 'aumākua. However, the author may be doing this merely to illustrate his point. Also, Queen Emma senses her dead husband and child as living presences and interprets this in Christian terms (Korn 1976:87).

I will not discuss other elements of chiefly religious ideology which continued through the nineteenth century and in some cases into the present. An example would be weather signs and omens for chiefs. See, e.g., *He Kanikau No Ka Moi Iolani Kamehameha IV!* "A Lament for King Kamehameha IV!" by Emma Lani (Queen Emma), Johnson 1976:252-55; *He Alii No Wau* "I am Indeed a Chief," a satirical song by Liliʻuokalani 1897:110, sts. 3, 5. See also below, pp. 22-23.

19. On the appropriation of legends, see Fornander 1969:23f., 32f. On genealogies, see ibid.:26ff.; cf. Kamakau 1961:243f., 394. See also David Malo Kupihea's accusation against Kalākaua of tampering with the text of the *Kumulipo* (Beckwith 1972:69f.).

20. See the section against the *haku mele* "composers" of the rival chief in *Haui Ka Lani* (Fornander 1919-1920:405f., ll. 670-701); Kamakau 1961:178.

21. E.g., Kamakau 1961:152f.; *Haui Ka Lani*, Fornander 1919-1920:390f., ll. 345-55; 392f., ll. 370-76. The genealogical controversy was especially important in the campaign between Queen Emma and Kalākaua (Korn 1976: e.g., 254-57, 264f., 268; Pratt 1920: 34f.). See also Liliʻuokalani 1964:43; Kuykendall 1953:243.

22. On prophets, see *Haui Ka Lani*, Fornander 1919-1920:407, l. 709. Johnson 1976:210, 212. This is also an element in later Hawaiian politics as in Korn 1976: e.g., 126, 186, 274. On sorcerers, see *Haui Ka Lani*, Fornander 1919-1920:392, ll. 360f. Kamehameha I was careful to gather to himself the famous poison gods of Molokaʻi (Summers 1971:15; Westervelt 1974:108f., 114f.; Westervelt 1975:33). Sorcery can be found later (Korn 1976: e.g., 189, 190, 200, 288ff.). See below, pp. 22-23.

23. *Haui Ka Lani*, Fornander 1919-1920:398, l. 495.

24. See Charlot 1973, 1979a, 1979b, 1982. I will not discuss problems of historicity here.

25. Fornander 1919-1920:391, l. 349. References for other points have been given above.

26. Ibid.:382-86, ll. 218-81; 407, ll. 710-33.

27. Ibid.:397, ll. 472-80; 400, ll. 524-32.

28. Charlot 1977:495-98; Charlot 1979b; Charlot 1983:26-29. To the references cited in Charlot 1977, add Rémy 1862:98 (warrior qualities), 58 (religious qualities), 94 (blame of Kiwalaʻō for hostilities); Keakaloloa, *He Wahi Moolelo no Kamehameha* "A Story of Kamehameha," in Fornander 1918-1919:688-93. Later literature could present the wis-

dom, peace, and beneficence of Kamehameha I's rule as a historical fact, rather than a prophecy (e.g., Rémy 1862:108-16; *Moolelo Pokole no Kamehameha I* "Brief History of Kamehameha I," cited and discussed in Charlot 1977:477, 479; Johnson 1976:214 [note the use of pono]). The genealogical ambiguity surrounding Kamehameha I's father has its source, I believe, in deliberate rumors spread for propaganda purposes: parentage was claimed from an earlier chief of the group to be conquered, thus establishing a legitimate claim for Kamehameha I (see, e.g., Nakuina 1904:18; McKinzie 1983:91).

29. Very little anti-Kamehameha literature remains, but see Pratt 1920:21f., 24ff., 28, 44-49. Even she admires, however grudgingly, Kamehameha's civil policy (ibid.:45f., 61). For the later idealization of Kamehameha, see, for example, Johnson 1976:164.

30. See above, n. 21. Also Korn 1958:96; Westervelt 1977:65; McKinzie 1983:63f., 66-69, 71, 95.

31. On the ceremony at Kamehameha's death, see Rémy 1862:124, 152. The only evidence I have found of Kamehameha being used as an 'aumakua is mentioned in note 18. On anniversary ceremonies, see Stewart 1970: 114-20. Cf. Rémy 1862:198f. Kepelino seems to be describing this ceremony as an old custom (Beckwith 1932:165).

32. Rémy 1862:202-4. The thinking of this chant was influential. See, e.g., L., W. C., *Ke Aupuni Hawaii* "The Hawaiian Government," in *Ka Nupepa Kuokoa*, 16 August 1862, p. 1; Johnson 1976:281; p. 21, below. Cf. Kamakau 1961:252, 256.

The use of '*imi* "search" to describe Kamehameha I's activity can be found during his lifetime (*Haui Ka Lani*, Fornander 1919-1920:389, l. 330; Kamakau 1961:151). The Hawaiian text of Kamehameha's statement (ibid.) reads:

Kupanaha! Kupanaha! hele mai nei hoi e imi i mau keiki hou, haalele aku nei ia oukou i na keiki makahiapo. Aloha ino!

33. Kamakau 1961:279. Cf. Pukui 1983: no. 553. A certain meritocracy is recognized in Kamehameha I's regime in that he employed the talented despite their racial or social origins. See Kamakau 1961: 374f.; Johnson 1976:214.

34. Kalākaua 1972:398. On Kamehameha I's farming, often mentioned in literature (e.g., Pukui 1983: no. 278), see Handy and Handy 1972:307, 309, 477f., 484f., 524, 529ff., 572. Cf. ibid.:534; Sterling and Summers 1978:47, 222, 300. Cf. also Fornander 1919-1920:468; Kamakau 1961:192.

35. On the oceanic empire as a basis for immigration policy, see Varigny 1874:310f.; see also ibid.:37. With respect to its role in foreign affairs, Varigny (1874:200f.) states that he used the precedent of Kamehameha I's plan to project a gradual attachment of the island groups of the South Pacific to Kamehameha V, either as king or protector. Horn (1951:3f., 61) found no adequate evidence for the influence of Kamehameha I's alleged plan on later politics, but he does not cite Varigny. Paul E. Hooper's *Elusive Destiny, The Internationalist Movement in Modern Hawaii* (University Press of Hawaii, 1980) appeared too late to be used in this article. On Kalākaua's suggestion of an Asian-Pacific empire to the Emperor of Japan, see Armstrong 1977:15, 17; Kuykendall 1967:156, 229f. Kalākaua's suggestion may have had an influence on later Japanese policy. In October 1914, the Japanese governor of occupied Saipan made the following address to a group of exiled Samoan chiefs (McKay 1968:26):

I am astonished at all you have done today, for it is clear that you are a chiefly people, as the Japanese are. Although you have been exiled far from your home, you have received me courteously and pleasantly; that is evidence that you and we are of one blood. Japan is beginning now to drive all the white people out of the Pacific, back to their own part of the world, and so to leave the Pacific entirely to the brown people. You will see in future one united Government for all the brown people, and it will continue always under the rule of the one Emperor of Japan."

The tone of racial solidarity against Americans and Europeans is present also in the Emperor's letter to Kalākaua (Kuykendall 1967:229) and corresponds to views developed by Kalākaua during his voyage (Armstrong 1977: e.g., 126ff., 132f., 144ff.). See especially ibid.:146: "The royal Hawaiian replied that he had now discovered that his own people were Asiatics, and he hoped the Asiatic nations would become powerful and stand by one another."

36. E.g., Kuykendall 1953:243; Charlot 1979b. Kalākaua's search for the burial place of Kamehameha I must be understood in this context (Barrère 1975:65–70). Yet another aspect of the tradition is the use of Kamehameha I in origin stories (e.g., Green and Pukui 1936:128, 130; Titcomb 1972:10f.).

37. Such sayings are more important in Polynesian than in Western culture. The importance of such mottos in nineteenth-century Hawaiian politics is indicated by Kalākaua's speech at Lahaina, Maui, 13 April 1874, in which he repeats the mottos of several of his predecessors, starting with Kamehameha I, and then formulates one for his own reign (Kunimoto 1965:145f., 146). K., *He Mele no ka Hae Hawaii* "A Chant for the Hawaiian Flag" (*Ka Nupepa Kuokoa*, 11 January 1862, p. 1) also emphasizes the mottos of the different reigns. For an unfulfilled saying of Kamehameha I, see Kamakau 1961:187.

38. For the saying, see H. P. Judd 1930:40, no. 469. On its possible realization, see Rémy 1862:172; Kamakau 1961:401; Kuykendall 1953:243. See also n. 37 above; Samuel Kuahiwi's *Nā Aliʻi* "The Chiefs," in Elbert and Mahoe 1970:79f., st. 1, l. 4.

39. For the saying, see H. P. Judd 1930:39, no. 447. On its use as a battle exhortation, see Rémy 1862:150; Johnson 1976:426.

40. H. P. Judd 1930:38, no. 440; 39, nos. 448f.

41. Discussion in the ʻAhahui Pūlama ʻŌlelo Hawaiʻi, Waiʻanae, Oʻahu, of which I was a member, 23 September 1978. Similar interpretations were made by people contemporary with the saying, although the sea people were variously identified, for example, as Kahekili, Kamehameha I, or Westerners. See Nakuina 1904:53f.; Pukui 1983: no. 1772. On the historical circumstances of the saying, see Fornander 1919–1920:282–91; Fornander 1969:221, n. 2; Westervelt 1977:147f.

My own interpretation is that Kaʻōpulupulu is comforting his son by telling him it is better to lie in the sea because the land originally emerged from it: that is, in death, he is returning to the source. I would translate *no ke kai* "from the sea" as did Kahiolo (1978:123): *no ke kai mai ʻoe* "you are from the sea?" When Mr. Hiram Kahala settled in Kahana Valley, Oʻahu, he was given a similar teaching by long-time residents: if they did not care for the land, the sea would reclaim it.

For an earlier use of the Kamehameha I saying in politics, see the campaign song *Lanakila Iaukea* (Williamson 1976:149f., st. 2, l. 4). I will argue below that the saying is the basis for the use of the word pōkiʻi in several texts.

42. Rémy 1862:120, 122. The sentence was apparently left unfinished, but the next words, *ʻaʻole i pau* "it was not concluded," have been taken by some as the final part of the quotation, with the meaning that the work of Kamehameha I is not yet finished. A proverb in H. P. Judd (1930:41, no. 471) seems to be a variant secondary to the above.

43. Johnson 1976:214.

44. For the saying, see Kuykendall 1947:220. The saying can be interpreted with security from an earlier speech by Kamehameha III (Kamakau 1961:364). I give below the text from *Ke Au Okoa*, 18 February 1869, page 1:

Auhea oukou e naʻlii, a me na kanaka, a me na makaainana mai kuu Kupunakane mai, a me na kanaka o ka aina e.
E hoolohe mai oukou, ke hai aku nei au ia oukou ia [?] pilikia, ua pilikia au no koʻu hoopilikia [ʻia (?)] mai me ke kumu ole, nolaila, ua haawi a[u i (?)] ke ea o ka aina o kakou i lohe oukou. Aka, e mau ana no koʻu alii ana maluna o oukou, a ma ko oukou pono, no ka mea, ke [l]ana nei koʻu manao, e hoihoi ia mai ana o ka ea o ka aina, ke hooponopono ia mai n[o] kaʻu hana.

In 1849, passive resistance was used against the French (Richards 1970:333).

The Kamehameha paradigm for the standard practice of distinguishing between the central foreign government and its errant representative could be the Scheffer incident (Kuykendall 1947:56–59).

45. Charlot 1979b:40.

46. Rémy 1862:224 (prior to, but extremely near, the Kamehameha III saying), 234.

47. For the quote, see Williamson 1976:151, 153, l. 3. On the allusion, see Fornander 1918-1919:490. Compare the use of the allusion for a newspaper (Johnson 1976:187, ll. 9ff.).

48. Johnson 1976:416 (vs. Kalākaua).

49. Kuykendall 1967:524.

50. See above, n. 24.

51. Liliʻuokalani 1964:104f., 176, 178, for example.

52. Author of *Iā ʻOe e Ka Lā e ʻAlohi Nei*, Elbert and Mahoe 1970:55f., discussed below. See also Armstrong 1977:58f., 194, 281f.

53. For the text, see Noble 1964:31. For the song version, *Kalani Kawika*, by J. Kealoha, see King 1948:147.

54. See above, n. 52. Elbert and Mahoe state that the chant was composed in 1881 before the trip. Armstrong (1977:281f.) gives the return from it as the occasion of its composition. The second chant given by Armstrong (ibid.) also displays the themes under discussion.

55. The theme of the warrior is also present in the Kalākaua movement (Charlot 1979a and b). See also Armstrong 1977:77, 182, 249f., 252ff., 256.

56. I will discuss below the theme of the kapu in the Kalākaua literature. Elbert and Mahoe (1970:56) connect the trampling on others' kapus to the ideology of the chief. It can be connected also to the literature on the volcano goddess Pele, which seems to have had an influence on the Kalākaua literature. See below and Emerson 1915:228-31; 229, l. 40: *Lele kapu i kai* "Kapus fly to the sea"; also 229f., ll. 41-47.

57. Line 8 is the nexus between the two levels of meaning, sight/seeing and sexuality: *hene* is used for the mountain slope and the Mount of Venus; *waiʻolu* "cool water" is a traditional sexual symbol. The regeneration of the race was an important part of Kalākaua's

policy, as in Kunimoto (1965:145f.). Kalākaua's genital chant, *Ko Ma'i Hō'eu'eu* "Your Lively *Ma'i*" (Elbert and Mahoe 1970:67f.), is famous. Sexual rites rumored to have been performed in the palace might have been intended to stimulate the fertility of the people. The revival of the hula, closely related to sexuality, may have been connected to this aspect of Kalākaua's policy. Praise of the chief's sexuality is traditional: on Kamehameha, see *Haui Ka Lani* (Fornander 1919-1920:380, l. 192).

58. Emerson 1909:117. He speculates (pp. 116f.) that the chant is an old one that has been adapted to Kalākaua. The Kalākaua themes, however, pervade the chant, and its tight composition seems modern: the chant is framed by identical first and last lines and by the second and second to the last lines, which express the pua theme. For the use of earlier materials in campaign songs, see Williamson 1976:137-41.

59. I would include line 10—which speaks of Kalākaua's being covered in the cloak of *mamo* feathers—as an expression of the theme of shining. Feather cloaks were considered to glow (Pukui and Elbert 1971: see *'ōwela*). Such cloaks were also symbols of chiefly rank and thus connected to the theme of heights.

60. Cf. above, n. 56. The place names Wahinekapu and Uwēkahuna are used significantly to recall the Pele cult. See Pukui, Elbert, and Mookini 1974:216, 218. On the significant use of place names, see ibid.:266-77.

An early witness of Kalākaua's attitude toward the Pele religion can be found in Korn (1958:53). Before his trip around the world, religious rites of Pele and other gods were performed (Armstrong 1977:xixf.). Uwēkahuna, "The Wailing of the Kahuna" is also, I would argue, a taunt against the sorcerers who practiced against Kalākaua (see above, n. 22).

Hawaiian religion had never, of course, been completely suppressed. Kamehameha V was known to have patronized it. Kalākaua seems to have decided early to support certain aspects of Hawaiian religion. For instance, he established the Hale Naua to evaluate genealogies and collect traditions, one of which was the *Kumulipo*, which he published in Hawaiian and which was later translated into English by Lili'uokalani (Beckwith 1972:1f.). During his trip around the world he met sovereigns whose positions were supported by religious, genealogical teachings similar to those in Hawaiian religion (Armstrong 1977:126, 180, 189, 286f.). See especially page 85:

> From several remarks made by my royal master I suspected that the common belief of the Japanese in the divine origin of the Emperor had strongly affected him, and he was planning the culture of a similar belief among his own people regarding himself. The Chamberlain and I saw symptoms of his scheme in his declaration one day that the kings of Hawaii descended from the *akuas* (gods), but that the missionaries had denied it. To establish or revive this belief among his superstitious subjects would be a ringbolt to which he could fasten his throne. On his return home he attempted this as a means of strengthening the loyalty of his people to himself, which was never over-strenuous.

In Meiji Japan, which greatly impressed Kalākaua, such a religious tradition was being used as the ideological basis for the modernization of the country, demonstrating that the adoption of Christianity was not necessary for that process.

On other aspects of non-Christian religions, see Armstrong 1977:84, 101f., 169.

61. Pukui and Korn 1973:134-49, 221f.; Pukui 1983: no. 1904; see also no. 1889.

62. See Appendix 2.

63. See Kalākaua's *Ke Ali'i Milimili* "The Cherished One," (Pukui and Korn 1973:166f., l. 12) and Lili'uokalani (1897:60), *Ka Hae Kalaunu* "The Crown Flag" (st. 2, ll. 3f.) where she warns:

Mai noho a kii ae i ke kapu,
No na mamo ia a Keaweaheulu.

Do not act as if to take the kapu,
It is for the descendants of Keaweaheulu.

Keaweaheulu was the ancestor of the Kalākaua dynasty. See also *He Lei No Ka'iulani (1893)*, ll. 4, 16, 28, in Pukui 1976:103f.; Rose 1978:45–55.

64. Pointed out by Lynn Davis of the Bishop Museum.

65. Elbert and Mahoe 1970:39f.

66. Ibid.:44.

67. Ibid.:45f.; Charlot 1983:90ff. Cf. *He Lei No Ka'iulani (1893)*, in Pukui 1976:103f., l. 32. This personalism can be found in the contemporary, non-Kalākaua literature as well, for instance Nu'uanu's *Kaleleonalani, Queen Emma* (King 1948:142, chorus, ll. 2, 4). I do not have a date for the beginning of this trend.

68. Pukui and Korn 1973:150–55, 222ff. See *He Halialia, Kalakaua Ia Kapiolani* "A Remembrance, Kalākaua to Kapi'olani" (Poepoe 1891:17f.) for Kalākaua's innovative use of regular meter in Hawaiian poetry.

69. Violence against heads of state was on people's minds (Pukui and Korn 1973:151; Armstrong 1977:133, 206f.). Kalākaua stated several times that he thought his people as happy as or happier than any he studied on his trip (Armstrong 1977:164, 276).

70. An example is preserved, I would argue, in Poepoe (1891:1–4). The style is very similar to chants on occasions of death.

71. Pukui and Korn (1973:222) suggest that the rhetoric of royal addresses and proclamations is a stylistic basis for the chant. I find such a basis more acceptable for Kalākaua's *Ke Ali'i Milimili*, discussed below.

72. Pukui and Korn 1973:165–69, 224f.; Lili'uokalani 1897:124. See ibid.:123 for another, possibly earlier, version.

73. Pukui and Korn 1973:224f. The reference to the eight seas is traditionally Hawaiian (vs. Pukui and Korn); see Elbert 1959:272 and note; Pukui 1983: nos. 2199, 2224. Flags were used most often as signals in battle to announce truces or mark places of refuge. See, e.g., Fornander 1916–1917:577; 1918–1919:391, 395; Elbert 1959:209; Beaglehole 1967: 482f., 501, 541f., 545f., 562f., 589; Green and Pukui 1936:166f.; Bird 1966:96f.; Pukui 1983: no. 2600. But the flag or similar object as emblem of the chief also has precedents (e.g., Johnson 1976:182f.; Fornander 1919–1920:293, l. 61 and n. 53; Westervelt 1977:201). John Kaulia's song version of the chant *Liliu E* (King 1948:119) contains the addition (st. 6, ll. 1f.):

E o e Liliu i kou inoa
Ka hae kalaunu o Hawaii nei.

Respond, Lili'u, to your name [chant],
The crown flag of Hawai'i.

Lili'uokalani is thus identified with the flag. Cf. *Lanakila Iaukea* in Williamson 1976: 149f., st. 2, l. 5:

A welo e ka hae Iaukea

Let the Iaukea flag wave.

The Kalākaua dynasty used the flag in its ceremonial, and Kalākaua took the royal standard with him around the world (Armstrong 1977:9, 14, 19f., 27–30, 33, 83, 85, 87, 89). The national and dynastic flags were used at the unveiling of the Kamehameha I statue (Charlot 1979b). Of course, others also invoked the flag. See, e.g., King 1948:142, st. 1, l. 1.

74. Milimili is usually used of children, for instance, the deceased son of Kamehameha IV and Queen Emma (Johnson 1976:221, 224). It was used in a child's name chant, which was later adapted for Lili'uokalani: *He Inoa Nō Kīna'u* "A Name Song for Kīna'u" (Elbert and Mahoe 1970:45, l. 2). In Lili'uokalani's *Ike Ia Ladana*, 1887 (Lili'uokalani 1897:115, st. 3, l. 4) she seems to use the word to translate the affectionate greeting of Queen Victoria:

Eia mai ho'i a'u milimili

Here is my dear one.

The word is used of Queen Emma by Nu'uanu in his *Kaleleonalani* (King 1948:142, chorus, l. 4).

75. A nearly exact parallel can be found in the chorus of *Ka Hae Kalaunu* (Lili'uokalani 1897:60):

O ka wehi Kalaunu o ke Aupuni,
No na Lani eha i ka Moku,
No lakou nei Hae Kalaunu
E mau loa kona welo ana.

The decoration, the crown of the government,
Is for the four Chiefs of the island.
For them is this Crown Flag
May its waving last forever.

In all likelihood, Kalākaua was familiar with this song and echoes its chorus in lines 4–5 and 10–11 of *Ke Ali'i Milimili*.

76. For a parallel to this sense, see Fornander 1919–1920:468, l. 261; and above, pp. 2–3. Compare the famous saying *Nānā i ke kumu* "Look to the source"; the racialist election slogan *Nānā i ka 'ili* "Look to the skin"; and Lunalilo's use of *nānā:* God should look with aloha on his people (Johnson 1976:342). The same image, with the word *'ike*, is found in Lili'uokalani's satirical *He Alii No Wau* (1897:110, st. 4, ll. 3f.):

Pai ae no oe a kiekie
I ike ia e ka lehulehu.

You are indeed raised high
To be seen by the multitude.

77. Johnson 1976:396. The play on two senses of *nānā* is similar to that in *Ke Ali'i Milimili*. Lili'uokalani could not be looking to the people for direction because she is sending them home. She is asking them to trust her, follow her direction, and support her with their affection. Later she writes (Lili'uokalani 1964:32) that after the overthrow of the monar-

chy "such sentiments as 'Look to the people' have been substituted for the ancient injunction to 'Look to the king.' " Compare the statement by Kekuaokalani (Kamakau 1961: 224). The Hawaiian text reads: *E nana aku hoi au ia oe, a e nana mai hoi oe ia'u.*

78. Many such examples can be found, such as *He Mele Aloha no Kulanui* "A Loving Song for the Seminary" (Fornander 1919-1920:529f.), a graduation chant based on the traditional genre of birth chant. The other school songs (ibid.:530-33) are also examples of the adaptation of an introduced literary form. See Appendix 3 for texts, documents, and bibliographical information pertaining to this section.

79. The British anthem was of course not the only source of such ideas. The saying "God save the king" was used in politics as an exclamation (Johnson 1976:340). Kamehameha III styled himself king *no ka Lokomaikai o ke Akua* "By the Grace of God" (L. F. Judd 1928:178f.). The constant reference to *"our* king" is probably derived from the British anthem.

80. Some influence may have come from foreigners, who more easily conceived of Hawai'i as an entity, such as Lorenzo Lyons in his *Hawai'i Aloha* "Beloved Hawai'i" (Elbert and Mahoe 1970:42).

81.

	Lunalilo	E. O. Hall	*Kuokoa* paraphrase
Akua	st. 1, l. 1	—	*Pauku* 1, etc.
mau	l. 1, etc.	st. 1, l. 4, etc.	3
ho'omaika'i	l. 2	—	1
pōmaika'i	l. 2	st. 3, l. 6	—
Mō'ī	l. 3, etc.	st. 1, l. 2	*Pauku* 1, etc.
mālama	l. 5	—	3
kia'i	l. 5, etc.	—	3, 4
mākou	l. 6	st. 1, l. 1	1
ola	l. 7, etc.	—	1, etc.
inoa	st. 2, l. 1	st. 1, l. 1	2
mai luna	st. 3, l. 2	—	2
E mau kou ola nei	l. 4	st. 1, l. 4	—
Ke 'Lii o nā 'Lii	st. 4, l. 2	st. 3, l. 1: *Lii*	*Pauku* 4: *ke Ali'i nui o na 'Lii*
aloha	l. 3	—	*Pauku* 4
aupuni	l. 5	st. 1, l. 5	
lākou	l. 6	—	*Pauku* 4
Iā oe nō	l. 7	st. 3, l. 7	—

82. The following table does not include all words common to the anthems. A reading of the four in sequence reveals their extensive similarity. The standardization of vocabulary within a genre was traditional Hawaiian literary practice, applied in this case to an introduced form.

	Lunalilo	Lili'uokalani	*He Himeni*	*Hawai'i Pono'ī*
mau	st. 1, l. 1, etc.	st. 1, l. 5; ch., ll. 1f., 4; st. 2 l. 3; st. 3, l. 6	st. 3, ll. 2, 4	—

	Lunalilo	Lili'uokalani	He Himeni	Hawai'i Pono'ī
pōmaika'i*	l. 2	—	st. 1, l. 3	—
mana	ll. 1, 4	st. 1, l. 1; ch., l. 3; st. 3, l. 8	—	—
mālama	l. 5	st. 2, l. 1	—	—
kia'i	l. 5; st. 3, l. 5	st. 3, l. 5	—	—
ola	l. 7, etc.	ch., l. 4; st. 2, l. 8; st. 3, l. 7	st. 3, ll. 3f.	—
inoa	st. 2, l. 1	—	st. 2, l. 2	—
lei	l. 2	—	st. 2, l. 6	—
pale	l. 5	—	—	ch., l. 3
'ino	l. 5	—	st. 2, l. 5	—
pule	l. 6	composed as prayer	st. 3, l. 1	—
hāliu, māliu	st. 3, l. 1	st. 1, ll. 2f.	—	—
nānā	l. 2	—	—	st. 1, l. 2; st. 2, l. 2
pōki'i	l. 3	—	—	st. 2, l. 4
pua	l. 6	—	—	st. 3, l. 3
aloha	st. 4, l. 3	st. 2, l. 5	—	—
ea	l. 4	ch., l. 1	—	—
aupuni	l. 5	st. 3, l. 2	st. 2, l. 4	—

*Pōmaika'i along with ho'omaika'i are used often in political contexts, e.g., Johnson 1976:257, 260, 281, 340.

83. Note especially the Christian or Biblical terminology in st. 1, l. 4 (the image of God's "mighty hand" is Biblical, not traditional Hawaiian); st. 2, l. 4; st. 4, l. 2. The first line of the anthem appears to be based on the doxology of the Lord's Prayer in Hawaiian, *Na Himeni Haipule Hawaii* (1972:7). The image of 'ēheu "wings" is used curiously of the Hawaiian flag in an anonymous chant composed in its honor (*Ka Nupepa Kuokoa*, 1 January 1862, p. 1, l. 6). (A complete study of the poetry published in the newspapers of the time, with identification of authors, would contribute to our understanding.) I would translate *ola mau* (st. 4, l. 6) as "eternal life" or life after death. Lunalilo would be giving a Christian sense to the oft used *ola* "life"; the Hawaiian sense would be vigorous, fertile living on earth, as opposed to weakness, sickness, and death. See, e.g., *Iā 'Oe e Ka Lā*, Elbert and Mahoe 1970:56, l. 16. Lunalilo's stanza 3, line 4, repeats Hall's stanza 1, line 4, and has the clear sense of long life on earth. The line is also used in *He Himeni* (st. 3, l. 4). Lunalilo is characteristically using concepts from both cultures.

84. See Beckwith 1932:143.

85. Significantly, the word is used in Ellen Wright Prendergast's *Kaulana Nā Pua* "Famous Are the Flowers" (Elbert and Mahoe 1970:62ff., st. 4, l. 4).

86. An apparent difficulty for this interpretation is that the word *kāu* "your" in line 3 must refer to God, since the subject looks down *mai luna mai* "from above"; but *kou* "your" in lines 4–5 clearly refers to the king or prince. My interpretation, however, fits lines 1–3 into the pattern of the whole anthem: the reception of God's help from above. Lines 4–5 are simply a shift of reference, found often in the compositions under discussion (e.g., *Hawai'i Pono'ī*, st. 2, l. 3). On the other hand, the second version of Lunalilo's anthem clearly raises the status of the king. Stanza 2 of the second version is clearly based on stanza

3 of the first. The same word, *māliu*, is used for the turning of the king to his people as was used previously for the turning of God toward the king or prince. However, the king does not do this *mai luna mai*, and the word *lāhui* "race" or "people" is used, not pōki'i. For a solution to the problem of shifting the address from one person to another, see below, note 100.

87. *Haui Ka Lani* (Fornander 1919-1920:400, l. 536) uses pōki'i in the general sense of descendant. This passage predates the saying of Kamehameha discussed below.

88. See above, p. 6. For the clear use of pōki'i connected to this saying and used in a political song, see *Lanakila Iaukea* (Williamson 1976:150, st. 2, l. 4).

89. See above, p. 7.

90. Green 1923:30-33.

91. E.g., *He Kanikau no Liholiho. I Kona Holo Ana i Beritania* "A Dirge for Liholiho. On His Trip to Britain," in Fornander 1919-1920:435-38; 437, l. 118. The situation is apparently that the spirit of Liholiho is being urged to return from England to see his chiefs.

In his acceptance speech Lunalilo seems to distinguish—within the category of the *lehulehu* "the multitude"—between the *maka'āinana* "the people of the land" and his pōki'i, the nobles who were present (Johnson 1976:338). See also *He Inoa Wehi No Kalanianaole*, Lili'uokalani 1897:127, l. 2. The word could, of course, be used in its literal sense, for example, Elbert 1956:110 (pre-Kamehameha I); Elbert and Mahoe 1970:46, st. 2, l. 3 (Kalākaua depicted referring to Leleiōhoku). I have found only one unambiguous reference—a post-overthrow one—to commoners as pōki'i of the monarch (Lili'uokalani 1897:127, l. 16). Further extensions of pōki'i include newspaper readers (Johnson 1976:149).

92. *Ka Nupepa Kuokoa*, 8 February 1862, p. 1.

93. Johnson 1976:342.

94. Compare her *Queen's Prayer* (Elbert and Mahoe 1970:88f.) with its resemblances to her anthem and Lunalilo's.

95. This can be seen schematically in the vocabulary table above, note 82.

96. This accords with the missionary view, above, page 7.

97. The English translation of these lines given in Lili'uokalani (1897:2-2) is: "Give the King thy loving grace." But her translation was meant to be sung and is not literal (Smith 1955a:19). *Na'au* designates the "insides" that determine a person's actions.

98. See the use of lehulehu for a crowd composed of both commoners and nobles (Johnson 1976:338). In *He Alii No Wau* (Lili'uokalani 1897:110, st. 4, l. 4) is a similar, undifferentiated use of lehulehu. Compare J. (Koana) N. Wilcox's *Kamuela King* "Samuel King" (Elbert and Mahoe 1970:60, l. 4) where lehulehu refers to the electorate. Also *He 'Ohu Lei No W. H. Heen* by S.K.K. (Williamson 1976:146, l. 2).

Interestingly, in Lili'uokalani's English translation of her anthem (1879:2-2), only three ranks are given: King (st. 1, l. 8; st. 2, ll. 1-4; st. 3, l. 6); chiefs (st. 3, ll. 1f.); and "people" (st. 2, l. 7; st. 3, ll. 3, 6). This might have influenced *Hawai'i Pono'ī*.

99.

	He Mele Lāhui	He Himeni	Hawai'i Pono'ī
makua	st. 1, l. 1	—	ch., l. 1
Mai Hawai'i a Ni'ihau	st. 1, l. 7	st. 1, l. 5, Mai Hawai'i a Kaua'i	—
Nā li'i (chiefs)*	st. 3, l. 2	st. 3, l. 5	st. 2, l. 2
maka'āinana	st. 3, l. 3	st. 3, l. 6	—

*Compare Lunalilo's anthem, st. 4, l. 2

See also the table in note 82. The traditional Hawaiian elements have been accepted from Lunalilo and the themes of national unity and social organization from Lili'uokalani, but the Christian elements they both used are increasingly omitted.

He Himeni was clearly composed with both previous anthems in mind. Lines 1–4 of stanza 1 are based on Lunalilo's stanza 1, lines 1–3; and *He Himeni*, stanza 1, lines 4–6, on Lili'uokalani's stanza 1, lines 5–6. See also below, note 101. But *He Himeni* is curiously even nearer in structure to Hall's *Restoration Anthem:* they are both three stanzas long; the king is addressed in the first stanza; and God is mentioned only in the last. The emphasis is, however, strongly shifted to the king by dedicating the second stanza to him rather than to Admiral Thomas. *He Himeni* takes a whole line from Hall, see above, note 83. *He Himeni* (st. 2, l. 2) takes *inoa maika'i* from Hall (st. 2, l. 1).

100. See above, n. 83. Interestingly, the author of *He Himeni* eliminates the difficulty of Lunalilo's shift of addressee by referring to God in the third person. See above, n. 86.

101. Cf. *He Mele Lāhui Hawai'i*, st. 3, l. 5. The placement of the line in *He Himeni*, following *inoa* in the earlier part of the stanza, shows that the author is consciously basing his anthem on Lunalilo's.

102. See above, pp. 12–13.

103. Other Kalākaua themes are only suggested. The inoa of the chief (st. 2, l. 2) is a reference to genealogical rank. The theme of heights is hinted at in that the name enjoys victory (ll. 3f.)

    Maluna a'e,
    O ke aupuni nei,

    Over,
    This government . . .

104. The coupling of the words *mō'ī* and *ali'i* can be found in the governmental prose of the reign (e.g., Johnson 1976: 370, 372, 376, 380). Stanza 1, line 4, may have been added because of the requirements of the melody (Smith 1955b:15). However, the repetition does emphasize a theme of the anthem.

105. Stanza 2 presents two problems for interpretation. First, are the pua (l. 3) and the pōki'i (l. 4) to be identified with the ali'i of line 2, or do they refer to one or two different sets of people? I would argue that stanza 2 should be parallel to stanzas 1 and 3, each of which addresses itself to a single social rank (I have shown how important this theme was in the development of anthems). Stanza 2 is similar to stanza 1, in which the last two lines refer to the same person as in line 2. Also, pua is a word often, but not exclusively, used for chiefs in the political literature, especially in the Kalākaua literature (see above, pp. 9–10;

cf. *Nā Aliʻi*, Elbert and Mahoe 1970:80, st. 1, ll. 8, 10). Pōkiʻi is a term for chiefs in the Kamehameha I tradition (see above, p. 16. It may be pertinent that the anthem was first presented at a ceremony during which Kalākaua's younger brother, Leleiōhoku, was appointed regent while the king was in the United States; Liliʻuokalani has the king call him pōkiʻi and successor after his death; see above, n. 91). Finally, although all English translations must be used with caution, Liliʻuokalani's clearly refers to the nobility: for example, pōkiʻi is translated "younger descent" (Liliʻuokalani 1897:54). This is true also of the English translations in Editor, P.C.A. 1875:8; Thrum 1887:45; Emerson 1909:175; King 1948:30; Smith 1955b:15. The general understanding at the time was, therefore, that the stanza referred to the order of chiefs.

The second problem of interpretation is the reference of *kou* "your" (l. 3). The usual referent for the second person possessive in the anthem is *Hawaiʻi ponoʻī* (st. 1, l. 2; st. 3, l. 3). However, no good sense can be extracted from that reference for stanza 2, line 3. For instance, *Hawaiʻi ponoʻī* includes the lāhui, the non-noble, racial Hawaiians (st. 3, ll. 1f.). The nobles could not be considered pua and pōkiʻi of the lower classes. Also, *muli* implies sequence in time; the pua could not exist after *Hawaiʻi ponoʻī* had passed away.

A second possible referent is Kamehameha I, who is addressed in the chorus. That the nobles are his pōkiʻi and the pua after him fits perfectly into the Kamehameha I tradition. The remaining difficulty—the awkward switch of referents between lines 1 and 3—is paralleled in the Lunalilo anthem (see above, n. 87) and elsewhere. In conclusion, stanza 2 refers to the order of nobles, although the switch between addresses to *Hawaiʻi ponoʻī* and Kamehameha I is awkward.

106. Lāhui was used for those below the king in Lunalilo's second version of his anthem (st. 2, l. 6). Thus it corresponded to the "we," the only group mentioned beside God and the king (see above, p. 17). In the title of Liliʻuokalani's anthem, lāhui could refer to the whole nation, including the king, under God. In *Hawaiʻi Ponoʻī*, the word is clearly not used in this inclusive sense. The duty of the lāhui is to ui, which, as will be seen, is inappropriate to the king. The word seems to be used, just as could be expected, to refer to the third and lowest order in a tripartite social scheme. For this sense, see Pukui 1983: no. 1937. Moreover, Kalākaua's motto, *Hoʻoūlu lāhui* "Increase the race," used the word in an obvious racial sense: he wished to reverse the declining birth rate among native Hawaiians. The use of lāhui in a racial sense would accord with *He Himeni* and Kalākaua's general policy. The last line of his *Ka Momi* is clearly racial: lāhui is modified by *kānaka*, a word used for the Hawaiian as opposed to the *haole* "non-Hawaiian" (Pukui and Korn 1973:154). Other clear examples of this racial use of lāhui can be found: for example, the *lāhui ponoʻī* of Queen Emma (Johnson 1976:284); *Lanakila Iaukea* (Williamson 1976:149, st. 1, ll. 3f.). Emerson (1909:172) calls *Hawaiʻi Ponoʻī* "the last appeal of royalty to the nation's feeling of race-pride."

In the summer of 1977 at Waiʻanae, Oʻahu, I asked a class on Hawaiian religion what *Hawaiʻi ponoʻī* meant. One of the religious leaders of the Hawaiian community replied forcefully, "Full blood!"

Consciousness of race was usual even among those whose politics were not racialist, for instance, Liliʻuokalani (1964:38, 83f., 97, 173, 195, 239, 255, 310, 315, 325ff., 366-73).

107. The expression may be traditional (Nakuina 1904:18). Compare the chant for the Hawaiian flag (*Ka Nupepa Kuokoa*, 1 January 1862, p. 1, l. 4): *Me ka Ihe i ka lima, a me ka ikaika pu*. Spear imagery can be found in other areas of contemporary culture. Spears guard the crown above the windows of the throne room in ʻIolani Palace. A prominent spear was placed in the hand of the statue of Kamehameha I and referred to in speeches and poems (Charlot 1979a and b). On earlier ceremonial uses of spears, see Richards 1970:230 (the spear of Kamehameha I), 283f. *Pale* (chorus, l. 3) was used in Lunalilo's

anthem (st. 2, l. 5). Cf. *Na Mele Aimoku* 1886:5, l. 16; 7, l. 2: these lines may belong to Ke'āulumoku's *'Au'a 'Ia* (see above, n. 7).

108. E.g., *Na Himeni Haipule Hawaii* 1972:6f.; Johnson 1976:342. Lili'uokalani (1897:54) translates the line:

Father above us all,
'T was Kamehameha,
Who guarded us from war . . .

She thus ignores the vocative of line 2 and the dual inclusive second person pronoun of line 3. Note also how the war theme is transformed into one of the prevention of war, in keeping with the emphasis on peace in her own anthem. See also H. L. Sheldon's translation in Thrum (1887:45):

O Thou who reign'st above,
Father of might and love!
Grant that thy peaceful dove
Brood o'er our land.

Emerson (1909:175) introduces Christianity more subtly into his translation:

Protector, heaven-sent,
Kamehameha great . . .

109. Fornander 1919-1920:371, l. 46; 372, l. 55; cf. 377, l. 137.

110. Pukui 1976:104. See above, p. 21. The same use of makua can be found in the satirical *He Alii No Wau* (Lili'uokalani 1897:110, st. 2, l. 4). Compare McKinzie (1983:1), and the use of makua for the first Christian or Christian-tending chief(s) in line 7 of *Ke 'Li'i ke Ola Mau* (Pukui and Korn 1973:33f.).

111. See above, page 6, for the idea of Kamehameha I as 'aumakua. How far Kalākaua entered into that idea is unclear.

112. A remarkable conceptual and linguistic parallel to Kalākaua's view is found in a speech by Kamehameha V (Johnson 1976:256). I have not, of course, presented a full discussion of theocentric vs. regiocentric viewpoints during the monarchy period, but merely studied them as they influenced the anthems. For instance, Lili'uokalani (1964:20f.) expresses an activist view of a monarch, although that is not the view expressed in her anthem.

113. Lili'uokalani's translation, "Younger descent" (see above, n. 105), seems to reflect the genealogical disputes of the time as to which lines were closest to Kamehameha I.

114. Compare, for example, Lili'uokalani 1897:54:

Duty calls fealty,
Guide in the right.

Emerson 1909:175:

With loins begirt for work,
Strive with your might.

King 1948:30:

Thy only duty lies
List and abide.

Notes 71

Smith 1955b:15:
   Thy great duty: Be loyal!
Elbert and Mahoe 1970:44:
   Your great duty
   Strive.
"Strive" does not correspond to the Pukui and Elbert (1971) definition of ui (2): "To stir up, activate."

115. Pukui and Elbert 1971: ui (1).

116. See above, pp. 13-14.

117. There is a certain lack of clarity in the relationship between Hawai'i pono'ī and the three orders of society. Hawai'i pono'ī seems to be used as both an all-inclusive and a selective term: that is, it seems both to include all the orders and, at the same time, to select the loyal individuals from within each order. This lack of clarity is the result, I would argue, of the fact that the phrase Hawai'i pono'ī addresses itself to the problem of unity; and the picture of the three orders addresses itself to the need for a simplified conception of society. The solutions to the two problems are joined without being synthesized.

118. The table below is based on the following texts:

   He Lei no Ka'iulani (1893). See above, nn. 63 and 67.
   Kalaniana'ole, ca. 1902, by Ernest K. Ka'ai. See above, n. 47. On the author, see Todaro 1974:162; Kanahele 1979:193ff.
   Lanakila Iaukea, ca. 1906–1908, by Ernest K. Ka'ai. See above, nn. 41, 73, 88, 106.
   He Wehi a he Lei no Kalama, ca. 1923, by Alani Hikina. Williamson 1976:144f.
   Kamuela King, 1936, by J. (Koana) N. Wilcox. See above, n. 98.
   Kaulana Nā Pua, 1893, by Ellen Wright Prendergast. See above, n. 85.

Further examples can be found in Williamson 1976, especially:

   Mele No Wilikoki, 1900, by David Umi. Williamson 1976:150f.
   He Inoa Keia No Ha'eha'e, 1923, by Helen K. Davis. Williamson 1976:147.
   He 'Ohu Lei No W. H. Heen, 1923, by S.K.K. See above, n. 98.

I will refer to these texts by title in the following notes.

	Ka'iulani	Kalani-ana'ole	Iaukea	Kalama	Kamuela King	Kaulana
ali'i	ll. 15, 21	—	—	—	—	—
alo	l. 19	—	st. 2, l. 4	—	—	—
aloha	ll. 14, 30f.	l. 24	st. 1, l. 1; ch., l. 2	l. 12	l. 6	st. 5, l. 5
ea	ll. 6, 14	—	—	—	—	—
ēwe	l. 30	—	st. 1, l. 4	—	—	—
inoa	—	—	—	—	ll. 1, 9	—
kalaunu	ll. 2, 10, 24, 34	l. 9	—	—	—	st. 5, l. 3
kia'i	—	l. 20	—	—	—	—
kōkua	—	l. 26	—	—	l. 7	—

	Ka'iulani	Kalani-ana'ole	Iaukea	Kalama	Kamuela King	Kaulana
kupuna	l. 30	ll. 10, 18	—	l. 19	—	—
lāhui	ll. 4, 22, 29	ll. 22, 27	st. 1, l. 3	l. 2	ll. 2, 10	—
lanakila	—	ll. 1, 12, 28	st. 1, l. 5	ll. 9, 22	—	—
lei	title; ll. 1, 15, 35	ll. 8, 18	ch., l. 1; st. 2, l. 2	l. 24	—	—
makua	l. 27	l. 17	—	—	l. 7	—
mālama	—	l. 22	—	—	—	—
mamo	—	l. 12	st. 2, l. 2	—	—	—
mana	—	l. 24	—	ll. 19f.	l. 8	—
mau	l. 32	—	—	—	l. 7	—
milimili	—	l. 8	—	—	—	—
noho	ll. 10, 24	—	—	l. 5	—	—
ola	ll. 3, 20, 36	l. 27	—	—	—	—
pōki'i	—	—	st. 2, l. 4	—	—	—
pono	—	l. 1	—	l. 3	—	st. 3, l. 4; st. 5, l. 2
pono'ī	—	—	st. 2, l. 3	—	—	—
pua	—	l. 9	—	—	l. 3	title; st. 1, l. 1
pu'uwai	l. 31	l. 6	st. 1, l. 2	—	—	—
wohi	ll. 4, 28	l. 22	—	—	—	—

119. I will discuss several such themes in the text. See, for example, the reference to the flag in such texts as *Ke Ali'i Milimili* (above, p. 13); *Lanakila Iaukea*, st. 2, l. 5; *He Wehi a he Lei no Kalama*, l. 9 (cf. l. 21); *Mele No Wilikoki*, st. 1, l. 4.

The theme of unity is often expressed by the word *lōkahi* "unity, agreement, accord" (Pukui and Elbert 1971): *Kalaniana'ole*, l. 5; *Lanakila Iaukea*, chorus, l. 2; *He Wehi a he Lei no Kalama*, l. 3; *Kamuela King*, l. 6.

As earlier—*He Mele Lāhui Hawai'i*, st. 1, l. 7; *He Himeni*, st. 1, l. 5; *Ke Ali'i Milimili*, ll. 1–4—the islands can be referred to or called upon in traditional terms: *Kalaniana'ole*, ll. 7, 11, 15, 19, 23; *Kaulana Nā Pua*, st. 2; *Kamuela King*, l. 5; *Mele No Wilikoki*, sts. 1–3, 5. For prose examples, see Poepoe 1891:1; Johnson 1976:415.

120. For example, more explicit appeal for votes can be found in the use of such words as:

moho "candidate": *Lanakila Iaukea*, st. 1, l. 6; *He Wehi a he Lei no Kalama*, ll. 2, 22; *Mele No Wilikoki*, st. 1, l. 1; *He Inoa Keia No Ha'eha'e*, ll. 2, 10, 14; *He 'Ohu Lei No W. H. Heen*, l. 2.

koho "vote": *He Wehi a he Lei no Kalama*, l. 3; *He 'Ohu Lei No W. H. Heen*, l. 7.

pāloka "ballot, vote": *Kalaniana'ole*, l. 5.

'elele "delegate": *Kalaniana'ole*, l. 1; *Mele No Wilikoki*, st. 1, l. 2; st. 6, l. 3; *Kamuela King*, ll. 2, 10; cf. *Kaulana Nā Pua*, st. 1, l. 3.

The phrase *aloha 'āina* and its variations, although present earlier (e.g., Emerson 1915:199, l. 12 of the Hawaiian text; Johnson 1976:350 [1874]; cf. Kamāmalu's chant, above, p. 6), seem to be used more frequently in this period (Johnson 1976:387, 416; Lili'uokalani 1897:126–29 [formulaic ending of this series of songs]; *Kaulana Nā Pua*, st. 5, l. 5; *Lanakila Iaukea*, st. 1, l. 1). The Hui Aloha Aina seems to have been founded at this time (Lili'uokalani 1964:301, 303). Compare *aloha lāhui* "love of the people/race" and its variations: Johnson 1976:256 (*ka poe aloha i ka lahui*, 1864); 281 (1865); Lili'uokalani 1897:126, l. 10 (first section). See also Charlot 1979c.

Notes 73

The word *hewa* "wrong" is used in several ways in the literature of the time. In *Kaulana Nā Pua* (st. 3, l. 3) it describes the "selling out" of the land. In *He Lei no Kaʻiulani (1893)* (l. 8) Kaʻiulani is pictured asking how she did wrong that her responsibility for governing has been denied her. Liliʻuokalani (1897:126, ll. 9f., first section) tells the imprisoned Prince Kūhiō Kalanianaʻole that his only wrong was his aloha for his race.

121. See above, p. 11. In l. 28, the theme of seeing the chief recalls *Ke Aliʻi Milimili*; see above, p. 13.

122. See, e.g., H. P. Judd 1930:36, no. 409; Charlot 1977:498ff. Cf. l. 30.

123. See above, p. 6.

124. See also the series of songs in Liliʻuokalani (1897:126-29) with the formulaic ending:

Hoʻokahi puana koʻu puʻuwai
No na poʻe i aloha i ka ʻāina.

A single refrain of my heart:
For those who love the land.

125. See above, pp. 11-12.

126. See, for example, Kalākaua's songs *Sweet Lei Lehua* (st. 1, l. 1) where puʻuwai refers to the loved one; also *Aloha No Au I Ko Maka* (st. 2, l. 4), in King 1948:41, 136.

127. See above, nn. 118, 124. Also *Mele No Wilikoki*, st. 6, l. 2; *He Inoa Keia No Haʻehaʻe*, l. 6 (the people); *He ʻOhu Lei No W. H. Heen*, l. 10.

128. See previous references. *Pulapula*, l. 20, is often used in pre-Christian prayers. The heights theme can be found in ll. 2, 21.

129. See previous note. Also, *poni ʻia* "anointed" (l. 26) can be used for "crowned." The feather cape (l. 10) is a chiefly emblem. *Mamo* "offspring" (l. 12) is a term used in chiefly genealogies.

130. See above, n. 127. See also milimili, l. 8, in *Kalanianaʻole* (used also in *Mele No Wilikoki*, st. 5, l. 2); *Hiʻipoi*, l. 16; *hiwahiwa . . . a ka makua*, l. 17 (cf. *Hiʻilawe*, Elbert and Mahoe 1970:49, l. 7; also, line 18 of *Kalanianaʻole* is literally line 8 of *Hiʻilawe*). The above words lend a similar private tone to others such as lei, lines 8 and 18, and pua, line 9. The poem is successful at projecting simultaneously a noble, traditional formality and an affectionate intimacy.

131. Line 24 seems to refer to the sorcery gods of Molokaʻi. A curious Christian parallel to the line can be found in Liliʻuokalani (1897:126, l. 9, second section):

E na Mana Lani e aloha mai

Oh heavenly Powers, give us your aloha.

132. See previous references.

133. Liliʻuokalani expressed her bitterness at the role played by Christian missionaries and their descendants in the problems and eventual overthrow of the monarchy (Liliʻuokalani 1964:9, 20, 37, 75f., 177f., 180-83, 188f., 231-34, 241, 244f., 257f., 269, 284f.). The lack of Christian references in these aristocratic works might be attributable to such a sentiment.

134. On the use of sorcery in politics, see above, pages 3–4. The use of *'enemi* (l. 11) and *loko'ino* (l. 12) for his adversaries may have been suggested by *Kaulana Nā Pua* (st. 1, l. 3; st. 3, l. 2).

135. See previous references. Also, the *kaulana* opening is paralleled by *Kaulana Nā Pua* (st. 1, l. 1) and *Mele No Wilikoki* (st. 1, l. 1); *hi'ipoi*, line 4, by *Kalaniana'ole* (l. 16); line 6 by *Lanakila Iaukea* (chorus, l. 2); line 8 by *He Wehi a he Lei no Kalama* (l. 20) and by *Lanakila Iaukea* (chorus, l. 3).

136. E.g., above, n. 82.

137. See Williamson (1976:137–44) for the habitual use of traditional forms.

138. See previous references and Charlot 1979c:6f.

139. For instance, palapala can refer to an academic degree, which is required for teaching but not possessed by many Hawaiians more knowledgeable than the non-Hawaiians occupying paid positions. The palapala can thus be described in the same line as *pākaha* "cheating, robbery, the taking unfair advantage of," and so on.

140. See, e.g., *Ka Hopena O Ke Pi* "The Result of Stinginess," in Green and Pukui 1936:118f.

141. The selling of Hawaii was discussed and attempted through the nineteenth century. See G. P. Judd 1960:208; Korn 1958:63f.; Armstrong 1977:xxiv, 256.

142. See above, n. 120.

143. Mrs. Mary Lee, a Hawaiian spiritual and community leader of Moloka'i, interprets the edible rock as the manna (Exodus 16) that would turn to rock if not eaten promptly as commanded by God. I have not found a Biblical text to support the view that the manna would turn to stone. Exodus 16:20 states that stored manna would develop worms and a bad odor. Mrs. Lee's interpretation may be based on a sermon tradition in a Hawaiian Christian church. Mrs. Jan Merryman has reported to me the opinion of Mrs. Pilahi Pākī that the song refers to food gathered on reefs: crabs, shellfish, seaweed, and so on. Such food clings to the coral or is caught by overturning submerged rocks. Mrs. Merryman said that the point of the song was that the government had taken over the land, forcing Hawaiians to go to the ocean to gather their food. Similarly, other informants have identified the rock with an artificial underwater rock pile built for fish to live in, or with a *kū'ula*, a god stone that attracts fish.

Some interpretations do not identify the *'ai* "food" with the *pōhaku* "rock." The lines would then refer simply to the land and the food grown from it. An argument against this view is that the song early received the alternative title *Mele 'Ai Pōhaku* "The Song of Eating Rock." Mrs. Bernice Auwana identifies the rock as the Rock of Revelation, a Mormon teaching, or as Jesus, the Rock of Ages; the 'ai is Hawaiian food. A full discussion of the lines would necessarily include an investigation of the places of both eating and rocks in Hawaiian culture and thinking.

Homer A. Hayes communicated privately to me the following notes on the passage under discussion:

> My mother, Flora Ka'ai Hayes, told me that "the Hawaiians would rather eat salt than knuckle under." (Salt and poi were common when *nothing* else was available.)
> Rem[ember]: Hawaiians would rather be impoverished than prosper under injustice. When they are nuha they get stubborn. "Nuhaism": "stubborn resistance."

Ancient belief: you cannot starve a Hawaiian to death as long as he had salt and poi left.

144. See Charlot 1979c. This view is supported by the report of the occasion of the song's composition (Elbert and Mahoe 1970:63).

145. *Mele O Kahoolawe* "Song of Kahoʻolawe" (1976, by Harry Kunihi Mitchell and Ruth Aulani Leighton, Poki Records 7410, text enclosed in record jacket) is a protest song against the use of the island of Kahoʻolawe as a target by the U.S. military. It is based on the genres of songs in praise of places and songs in praise of people. The island is greeted with aloha. Its *inoa* "name" is *mai kinohi* "from the beginning," a choice of words inspired perhaps by Genesis 1:1 of the Hawaiian Bible. The older name incorporates that of the god Kanaloa. The young Hawaiians, the pua, occupy the island bringing it peace, *hoʻomalu*. They struggle with the *aupuni* "government," firmly united in their desire for *ka pono o ka ʻāina* "the right of the land." They are urged forward, *imua*, to victory, *lanakila*, for the island. The lāhui is urged to work together from the rising to the setting of the sun, a spatial reference to the islands as a whole as well as a temporal reference. The *kānaka* "Hawaiians" are urged to strengthen themselves. They are few, but *ke aloha no ka ʻāina* "the love for the land" is great.

Many of the terms and themes of this song are clearly based on earlier works such as those discussed in this article.

146. Liliʻuokalani 1964:367. For Kepelino, see Charlot 1983:116ff.

147. Ibid.:368.

148. Ibid.: e.g., 83f., 195.

149. See, for example, Liliʻuokalani (1964:196) speaking of the *ʻōʻō* bird, which she was trying to save from extinction:

> These seemed to be thriving. Perhaps one cause of their content was a shrub or bush of the mimosa family growing near to the house, which bore fragrant blossoms very similar to those of the lehua, from which, in its own native island, this bird sucks the honey on which it subsists. They are true Hawaiians; flowers are necessary for their very life.

Liliʻuokalani's own sensitivity to nature is evident throughout the book (e.g., p. 319) and in her poetry.

150. Ibid.:53.

Glossary

aho nui: patience
'ai: food
akua: god
ali'i: chief
aloha: love
'ano: character, sense
'ānunu: greedy
'aumakua: family god, deified ancestor
aupuni: government

ea: life-breath
'ēheu: wing
'elele: delegate
'enemi: enemy

ha'awina: assigned lessons
hana nui: great work
haole: non-Hawaiian, white
Hawai'i pono'ī: Hawai'i's own
hewa: wrong
hilina'i: to believe

'imi: search
i mua: forward
inoa: name

kahuna: priestly expert
kamaha'o: wondrous
kanaka: human, Hawaiian as opposed to non-Hawaiian, subject as opposed to chief

kānāwai: law
kapu: tabu
kāua: we two
koho: vote
kōkua: aid, help
kua'ā: burning back
kuleana: responsibility
kūpa'a: to stand firm
kū'ula: god stone that attracts fish

lāhui: race, people
lanakila: victory
lani: firmament, chief
lawa: enough, sufficient
lehulehu: multitude
lōkahi: unity, agreement, accord

maka'āinana: person or people of the land
makua: parent; special sense: person used as genealogical basis for a claim
mālama: to care for
mālamalama: to shine
māliu: to turn to
malu: shade, shelter, peace
mamo: offspring
mana: power
mau: enduring
milimili: cherished one
minamina: to value, cherish, care for

moho: candidate
mōʻī: monarch

naʻau: insides, intestines
nānā: to look

ola: life
ola mau: eternal life

paʻa: firm, bound
palapala: document
pāloka: ballot, vote
pepa: paper, written documents

pōhaku: rock
pōkiʻi: younger brother
pōmaikaʻi: well-being
poni: to anoint, crown
pono: correct, right, righteous
pua: flower
puʻu: hill
puʻuwai: heart

ui: to ask, question, appeal

waiʻolu: cool water

Bibliography

Armstrong, William N.
1977 *Around the World with a King*. Rutland, Vermont and Tokyo: Charles E. Tuttle.

Barrère, Dorothy B.
1969 *The Kumuhonua Legends: A Study of Late 19th Century Hawaiian Stories of Creation and Origins*. Honolulu: Bishop Museum Press.

1975 *Kamehameha in Kona: Two Documentary Studies*. Honolulu: Bishop Museum Press.

Beaglehole, J. C., ed.
1967 *The Journals of Captain James Cook on His Voyages of Discovery*. Vol. 3, *The Voyage of the* Resolution *and* Discovery *1776–1780*. Cambridge: Cambridge University Press.

Beckwith, Martha Warren, ed.
1932 *Kepelino's Traditions of Hawaii*. Honolulu: Bishop Museum Press.

1970 *Hawaiian Mythology*. Honolulu: University of Hawaii Press.

1972 *The Kumulipo: A Hawaiian Creation Chant*. Honolulu: University of Hawaii Press.

Bille, Steen
1851 *Beretning om Corvetten Galathea's Reise omkring Jorden 1845, 46 og 47*, vol. 3. Copenhagen: C. A. Reitzel.

Bird, Isabella L.
1966 *Six Months in the Sandwich Islands*. Honolulu: University of Hawaii Press.

(Buda)
1904 *Mookaao Hawaii no Kahalaopuna, O ke Awawa o ke Anuenue*. Honolulu: Paredaiso o ka Pakipika.

Buke Mele na Ka Moi H. M. Kalakaua
n.d. Private Library, Iolani Palace, Archives of Hawaii, Genealogy Books Number 21 (G-21), Honolulu.

Charlot, John
1973 "The Arts." *Atlas of Hawaii*, pp. 126–30, 209. Department of Geography, University of Hawaii. Honolulu: University of Hawaii Press.

82 Bibliography

Kaeppler, Adrienne L., and H. Arlo Nimmo, eds.
1976 *Directions in Pacific Traditional Literature.* Honolulu: Bishop Museum Press.

Kahiolo, G. W.
1978 He Moolelo No Kamapuaa: *The Story of Kamapuaa.* Translated by Esther T. Mookini, Erin C. Neizmen, and David Tom. Hawaiian Studies Program, University of Hawaii.

Kalākaua, David
1972 *The Legends and Myths of Hawaii: The Fables and Folk-Lore of a Strange People.* Edited by R. M. Daggett. Rutland, Vermont and Tokyo: Charles E. Tuttle.

Kamakau, Samuel M.
1961 *Ruling Chiefs of Hawaii.* Honolulu: The Kamehameha Schools.
1964 Ka Poʻe Kahiko, *The People of Old.* Honolulu: Bishop Museum Press.
1976 *The Works of the People of Old,* Na Hana a ka Poʻe Kahiko. Honolulu: Bishop Museum Press.

Kanahele, George S., ed.
1979 *Hawaiian Music and Musicians: An Illustrated History.* Honolulu: University Press of Hawaii.

King, Charles Edward
1948 *King's Book of Hawaiian Melodies.* Honolulu: Charles E. King.
1950 *King's Songs of Hawaii.* Honolulu: Charles E. King.

Kirtley, Bacil F., and Esther T. Mookini, trans.
1977 "Kepelino's 'Hawaiian Collection': His 'Hooiliili Havaii,' Pepa I, 1858." *The Hawaiian Journal of History* 11:39–68.

Korn, Alfons L.
1958 *The Victorian Visitors.* Honolulu: University of Hawaii Press.

Korn, Alfons L., ed.
1976 *News from Molokai: Letters between Peter Kaeo & Queen Emma 1873–1876.* Honolulu: University of Hawaii Press.

Kunimoto, Elizabeth Nakaeda
1965 "A Rhetorical Analysis of the Speaking of King Kalakaua, 1874–1891." Thesis, University of Hawaii.

Kuykendall, Ralph S.
1947 *The Hawaiian Kingdom, 1778–1854: Foundation and Transformation.* Honolulu: University of Hawaii Press.
1953 *The Hawaiian Kingdom.* Vol. 2, *1854–1874: Twenty Critical Years.* Honolulu: University of Hawaii Press.
1967 *The Hawaiian Kingdom.* Vol. 3, *1874–1893: The Kalakaua Dynasty.* Honolulu: University of Hawaii Press.

Liliʻuokalani
1897 "He Buke Mele Hawaii I Haku Ponoi, Hoonohonoho a mahele ia e Liliuokalani o Hawaii, Wahinekona, Mokuaina o Kolumepia, 1897." Archives of Hawaii, Honolulu.

1964   *Hawaii's Story by Hawaii's Queen.* Rutland, Vermont and Tokyo: Charles E. Tuttle.

Lyons, Curtis J.
1875   "A Song for Kualii." *The Islander* 1:239-41.
1893   "The Song of Kualii, of Hawaii, Sandwich Islands." *The Journal of the Polynesian Society* 2:160-78.

McKay, C. G. R.
1968   *Samoana: A Personal Story of the Samoan Islands.* Wellington: A. H. & A. W. Reed.

McKinzie, Edith Kawelohea
1983   *Hawaiian Genealogies Extracted from Hawaiian Language Newspapers,* vol. 1. Laie: The Institute for Polynesian Studies.

Malo, David
1951   *Hawaiian Antiquities* (Moolelo Hawaii). Honolulu: Bishop Museum Press.

Mitchell, Harry Kunihi, and Ruth Aulani Leighton
1976   *Mele O Kahoolawe* "Song of Kahoolawe." Honolulu: Poki Records 7410.

Morris, Nancy Jane, Verna H. F. Young, Kehau Kahapea, and Velda Yamanaka
1974   *Preliminary Bibliography of Hawaiian Language Materials at the University of Hawaii, Manoa Campus.* Pacific Islands Program, University of Hawaii.

Na Himeni Haipule Hawaii
1972   Honolulu: Hawaii Conference, United Church of Christ.

Nakuina, Emma Metcalf
1904   *Hawaii, Its People, Their Legends.* Honolulu: Hawaii Promotion Committee.

Na Mele Aimoku, Na Mele Kupuna, A Me Na Mele Pono O Ka Moi Kalakaua I A Ua Pai Ia No Ka La Hanau O Ka Moi, Ke Kanalima Ponoi O Kona Mau Makahiki.
1886   Honolulu.

Noble, Johnny, ed.
1964   *Hawaiian Hulas.* New York: Miller Music Corporation.

Poepoe, Joseph M.
1891   *Ka Moolelo o ka Moi Kalakaua I.* Honolulu: Joseph M. Poepoe (?).

Pratt, Elizabeth Kekaaniauokalani Kalaninuiohilaukapu
1920   *Keoua, Father of Kings, History of Keoua Kalanikupuapa-i-kalani-nui, Father of Hawaii Kings, and His Descendants, with Notes on Kamehameha I, First King of All Hawaii.* Honolulu: Honolulu Star-Bulletin.

Pukui, Mary Kawena
1976   "Aspects of the Word *Lei.*" In *Directions in Pacific Traditional Literature,* Kaeppler and Nimmo, eds., 103-15.

1983   *'Ōlelo No'eau, Hawaiian Proverbs & Poetical Sayings.* Honolulu: Bishop Museum Press.

Pukui, Mary Kawena, and Samuel H. Elbert
1971   *Hawaiian Dictionary.* Honolulu: University of Hawaii Press.

Pukui, Mary Kawena, Samuel H. Elbert, and Esther T. Mookini
1974 *Place Names of Hawaii*. Honolulu: University of Hawaii Press.

Pukui, Mary Kawena, and Alfons L. Korn, trans. and eds.
1973 *The Echo of Our Song: Chants & Poems of the Hawaiians*. Honolulu: University of Hawaii Press.

Rémy, Jules
1859 *Récits d'un vieux sauvage pour servir à l'histoire ancienne de Havaii*. Chalons-Sur-Marne: E. Laurent.

1862 *Ka Mooolelo Hawaii: Histoire de l'archipel Havaiien (Iles Sandwich)* [Sheldon Dibble]. Paris and Leipzig: A. Franck.

Richards, Mary Atherton
1970 *The Hawaiian Chiefs' Children's School: A Record Compiled from the Diary and Letters of Amos Starr Cooke and Juliette Montague Cooke*. Rutland, Vermont and Tokyo: Charles E. Tuttle.

Rose, Roger G.
1978 *Symbols of Sovereignty: Feather Girdles of Tahiti and Hawai'i*. Honolulu: Bishop Museum Press.

Sinclair, Marjorie
1976 *Nāhi'ena'ena, Sacred Daughter of Hawai'i*. Honolulu: University of Hawaii Press.

Smith, Emerson C.
1955a "Know Hawaii's Songs: The National Anthems." *Paradise of the Pacific* 67 (March):18–19, 22.

1955b "Know Hawaii's Songs: The National Anthems, Part II." *Paradise of the Pacific* 67 (April): 14–15, 26.

Sterling, Elspeth P., and Catherine C. Summers, eds.
1978 *Sites of Oahu*. Honolulu: Bishop Museum Press.

Stewart, C. S.
1970 *Journal of a Residence in the Sandwich Islands, during the Years 1823, 1824, and 1825*. Honolulu: University of Hawaii Press.

Summers, Catherine C.
1971 *Molokai: A Site Survey*. Honolulu: Bishop Museum Press.

Thrum, Thos. G., ed.
1887 *Tributes of Hawaiian Verse, Second Series*. Honolulu: Thos. G. Thrum.

Titcomb, Margaret
1972 *Native Use of Fish in Hawaii*. Honolulu: University of Hawaii Press.

Todaro, Tony
1974 *The Golden Years of Hawaiian Entertainment*. Honolulu: Tony Todaro.

Varigny, C. de
1874 *Quatorze ans aux Iles Sandwich*. Paris: Hachette.

Westervelt, W. D.
- 1963 *Hawaiian Legends of Volcanoes*. Rutland, Vermont and Tokyo: Charles E. Tuttle.
- 1974 *Hawaiian Legends of Ghosts and Ghost-Gods*. Rutland, Vermont and Tokyo: Charles E. Tuttle.
- 1975 *Hawaiian Legends of Old Honolulu*. Rutland, Vermont and Tokyo: Charles E. Tuttle.
- 1977 *Hawaiian Historical Legends*. Rutland, Vermont and Tokyo: Charles E. Tuttle.

Williamson, Eleanor
- 1976 "Hawaiian Chants and Songs Used in Political Campaigns." In *Directions in Pacific Traditional Literature*, Kaeppler and Nimmo, eds. 135–56.

The Author

John Charlot was raised in the mainland United States, Mexico, and Hawai'i. He studied at Chaminade College, Harvard College, the University of Louvain, and the University of Munich, where he earned his doctorate in religious studies in 1968. He has taught in Minnesota, Sāmoa, Hawai'i, and Canada, and created a sequence of courses in Hawaiian and Polynesian religions at the University of Hawaii. He has published numerous scholarly and popular works on culture and religion, most recently *Chanting the Universe: Hawaiian Religious Culture* in 1983. He served as curator of the Jean Charlot Collection, Thomas Hale Hamilton Library, University of Hawaii, and is currently a research associate at the East-West Center, Honolulu.